A Guide To Effective Prayer

By
Phyllis Jemmott

Ministry In Art Publishing Ltd

e-mail: info@miapublishing.com

www.miapublishing.com

Unless otherwise stated, all scripture quotations are taken from the Holy Bible, New King James Version. Quotations marked NKJV are taken from the HOLY BIBLE, NEW KING JAMES VERSION. Copyright © 1973, 1978, 1984 by International Bible Society. Used by permission of Hodder and Stoughton Ltd, a member of the Hodder Headline Plc Group. All rights reserved. "NKJV" is a registered trademark of International Bible Society. UK trademark number 1448790.

Quotations marked KJV are from the Holy Bible,

King James Version.

ISBN Number: 978-1-907402-32-6

Cover Design: Allan Sealy

Contents

Preface

The aim of writing this book is to share the truth that I have discovered on my Christian journey. This book is intended for all age groups. It will become a useful tool in your hands and will act as a guide to the effectiveness of prayer. This book is presented to readers in an easy-to-understand manner, and can be used as a study guide, or as a reference book for pleasure, or for spiritual enlightenment.

When I started preparing the first draft, unfortunately it was destroyed. It was completely wiped out but I decided that it must be done, plucked up the courage and started putting things together again. It is such a delicate topic that all the devils in hell would resist me talking or writing about it.

The words in this book are bathed in prayer. I often sought the Lord with tears while searching God's word for explanations and clarity. I tell you it was worth it all, even with the tired eyes and fingers.

Today I want you to think not so much about who is the author, but of the contents of the book.

Guide to Effective Prayer will guide you into some insight of prayer and its significance. I hope that by taking the time to read this book it will serve as a mighty tool in the hands of every reader. I have tried to apply most, if not all, of the contents to my personal life. It will inspire you to rise up and pray, and seek guidance on how to pray effectively.

You will learn that prayer is the key to unlock closed doors; it is the answer to all life's problems. This book will give you guidance and assurance when feeling doubtful. It will help you build your faith and take hold of God's promises.

I have taken into consideration that most people are put off by long extracts of text, so I deliberately prepared this book with short chapters to make it more readable, without losing the important message of the book.

This book will allow you to dig deeper into the word of God. You will not only read about the benefits of effective prayer, but also how our prayers can be hindered through unbelief, sin, doubt, unforgiveness and many other factors.

You will find some exciting chapters about how people in biblical days won battles and gained victories through the medium of praying in faith. By reading and looking up scriptures that are stated in this book you will know how to exercise your faith, because faith comes by hearing the word of God. You also will find practical applications of how to use prayer arrows to hit areas that are ordinarily unattainable.

Pray your way beyond the veil and discover the refreshing presence of Almighty God. I encourage you not only to read this book but also to send a copy to a friend, a neighbor, and even an enemy.

May you experience heaven's blessing as you read and search the scriptures to find the cure for all the conditions in life that you may be experiencing.

I can now say 'Hither to have the Lord helped me'.

Happy reading.

Introduction

Jesus' disciples asked Him to teach them how to pray. He taught them a model prayer. It is often called '*The Lord's Prayer*'. It is a command by our heavenly Father that we should pray not only for ourselves but with and for others. We should pray only to God alone, and not to the saints or angels.

We observe what we were taught about the Lord's Prayer, and how to address ourselves to God, and the title we give Him when we pray. Also how to accept the invitation that He offers, to come boldly to the throne of grace, that we may find grace for the time of need. This invitation is for the unbelievers to believe and to accept. His compassion never fails; therefore He is able to supply all our needs according to His riches in glory by Christ Jesus *(Philippians 4: 19)*.

We must address ourselves to Him as Father and recognize that He is our Father. There is nothing more pleasing and pleasant than when we address God as our Father.

According to Psalm 103-13 He is truly our Father. He will pity us in our weaknesses and infirmities when we know not what we ought to pray for; He helps us with our uncertainties.

When we approach the throne of grace in repentance of our sins we must believe that God is able to cleanse and forgive us of all sins.

Reading from Matthew 6 verse 9, we discover some powerful verses in the form of a simple prayer. This prayer is like a letter sent from earth to heaven.

In Jesus' great model prayer we observe five stages: Adoration, with thanksgiving, petitioning, worship, praise, contrition and intercession.

In this book we will learn more about these stages of prayer, and how by employing these stages we can enrich our worship and more intelligently present to God the needs of others.

We will look at what prayer is, and how we can make our requests known to God.

We will see that every one has a need to pray, and should be encouraged to get engaged in active prayer life.

You will find different kinds of prayer, their requirements, and the reasons for unanswered prayers.

We will look at the importance of prayer and the church; if everyone in the church engaged themselves with commitment to pray what a bountiful outcome that would be!

Next we will read about building our own faith. Everyone has faith, but each person needs to build on what they receive.

We will learn about prayer arrows and how effective they can be: if more people would send out prayer arrows it would reach the lost for Christ.

Read about what is beyond the veil; now that it has been rend in twain we can now go to God through Jesus Christ at any time.

We also share a true story from a real mother, and how her faith in praying has given her great confidence concerning God's power to change the life of her son.

You will find the names of God with meanings and references. I personally find it fascinating.

And finally, we include some letters of commendation that were sent out in love to real people.

Join me in prayer.

Almighty God and our Father, I come to You in the name of Jesus Christ Your Son. I come to you upon the invitation that you have lovingly offered. Father, you have said that we should come boldly to the throne of grace where we can find grace for every need.

Lord, it is not any good that I have done to gain this privilege to come boldly to Your throne of grace. Father, it is only through Your loving kindness, and Your tender mercies toward me, that I am able to offer this prayer to you. You have been good to me more than how I have been good to myself, O Lord, I give you praise.

Father I thank you for cleansing me from sin. I ask You for continual awareness of Your divine presence, so that I may always keep my heart in perfect peace and my mind stayed on You. Truly Lord You are great and Your greatness is extended to all generations. I give You honor and praise.

As we begin to read through each chapter of this book, Lord, help me to draw inspiration from Your word so that every page will speak a message of deliverance and hope to my spirit.

I humbly ask these mercies in Jesus Christ's name.

Amen

1

Lord, Teach Us To Pray

Jesus had drawn away from His disciples for a quiet retreat; He took advantage of the seclusion to pray. While His followers were around him, they often watched Him pray. No doubt they would have seen His face rapt in devotion. The disciples constantly observed Jesus as He prayed. They sensed the presence of God and were awed by it. As Jesus finished praying, one of them voicing their desire said, 'Lord, teach us to pray'. The disciples had seen His mighty miracles but they did not ask for that power. They had heard His mighty preaching, but they did not ask Him how to preach. It was His prayer life, His communion with His Father that they longed to experience.

He responded to their request and proceeded to teach them how to pray. If Jesus responded so promptly to His apostles, He will, no doubt, respond to our sincere desires. Jesus was only too pleased to grant this request. He knew that once His followers developed a life of prayer they would become spiritual warriors to master any situation.

Prayer would grant them a humble heart, a child-like attitude and the understanding to deal with any crisis. Jesus knew that His disciples' eyes would be open to sin, and they would be more aware of how to shun the very appearance of evil. They would have an experience of how to communicate more effectively to God as their Father.

Jesus showed that His personal prayer life followed a pattern that can be exemplified by all His followers. He was always in prayer to meet the challenges and any crisis that He faced, because He was always sought

A Guide to Effective Prayer after either by His enemies or people that needed His cure. His prayer life was as a mighty weapon to ward off the attacks of His enemies. The Lord knew that the disciples would be crushed at the thought of Him leaving them, as they did not realize the full meaning of what He had told them about His death by the wicked hands of the people. They did not have any idea that He was about to leave them as orphans in a cold and unfriendly world. He was glad when they asked Him to teach them to pray.

Jesus made the prayer so simple, and yet so detailed. He included all that was necessary for their spiritual, physical, and emotional life in the prayer. While Jesus was with the disciples they had the privilege to ask Him anything, but when He left them, the Holy Spirit would come in to impart new life and equip the disciples to develop a strong prayer life.

Are you willing to be placed under His tuition? Are you prepared to master the lessons of effective prayer? If your answer is yes, then He is willing to guide you into effective prayer. Blessed are those who are willing to be taught, they will be good followers.

What Is Prayer?

Prayer is communication that is addressed to Jehovah the true God. It involves our devotion, trust, and respect. It is through petition and supplication that we make a request for help and pleading for pardon that is directed to God the Father and Jesus Christ the Son. Prayer is exercising one's faith in God, and believing that your prayers will be answered, and that any situation that we face can be met and rectified.

Prayer therefore includes confession (2 Chronicles 30:22); petition or request (Hebrews 5:7); and expression of praise and thanksgiving (Psalms 34:1, 92:1).

During our prayers we must also express adoration and worship as the most important elements in our prayer. It is imperative that we pray to God in the name of Jesus. We must realize that we are not praying to Jesus when we are praying, rather we are praying to the Father in the name of Jesus. It is Jesus who gives us the power of attorney, meaning that Jesus' name gives us the right to go into the presence of our Father God to make our request, and receive answers to our prayers.

Prayer is then a two-way conversation that will develop into a relationship with God. It will also improve our listening skills that we may hear what He has to say during our prayer time. Prayer is therefore like having a conversation with God because life is sustained by union and communion (see Ephesians 6:18 also 1John 5:14).

The disciples would often face difficult situations that could only resolve through prayer. Prayer is the key that unlocks faith in our lives. Effective prayer needs an attitude and dependency, an action, and asking. Prayer will demonstrate our reliance on God as we humbly invite Him to fill us with faith and power. There is no substitute for prayer in circumstances that seem impossible.

When Should We Pray?

It is absolutely necessary to pray at all times, praying time should be like the breath we breathe: we cannot live without it. The word of God says we should pray without ceasing. Therefore prayer should be a lifestyle. That means we are to pray as often as the opportunity arises.

We are all responsible for making our own time to pray. The Spirit of God will urge the believer that it is prayer time. We should listen to the Spirit and obey. We may never know or understand when the Spirit invites us to pray at a particular time. Someone can be facing serious trouble and in need of prayer of deliverance. Prayer should therefore be a matter of urgency, and expectancy. We can pray spontaneously. We can pray even while talking to others. Believers know that God is always present and hears and answers every prayer that we pray in faith. Nehemiah prayed confidently throughout the day, because he had established an intimate relationship with God during times of extended prayer. If we want to reach God with our prayers we need to take time to cultivate a strong relationship with God through times of prayer.

And this is the confidence that we have in him, that, if we ask any thing according to His will, He hears us (1 John 5: 14).

Where Should We Pray?

Men must pray everywhere, no place is amiss for prayer, and no place is unacceptable to God. We must lift up holy hands and pure hearts from the pollution of sin. We must pray in charity without wrath or malice. Considering where we should pray is a matter of choice. The word of God encourages us to go to our closet and shut the door since it is a place with few distractions, where we can be alone with God.

Jonah the prophet prayed in the belly of the big fish. This prayer was a prayer of thanksgiving that he had not drowned in the sea instead. But even from where he found himself, he remembered God, he cried out to God for help. God saw him, heard him, and delivered him (see Jonah 1:2). In the Old Testament days, the Jews usually went to the Temple for prayer, but in the New Testament days, men commonly prayed to God anywhere.

I heard about a brother who gave his testimony that it was while he was in his field working that he prayed to receive the baptism of the Holy Ghost. The Lord saw how much he was desperate to be blessed, and gave him what he asked for. It is possible that even while we are walking, driving or working we can say a silent prayer until we can arrange the closet sessions with God. We must create an atmosphere where we can set aside quality time to be alone with God in prayer, coupled with faith without wavering. There is no predicament that is too hard for God.

What Should We Pray About?

First and foremost, we should confess to God all known sins, and ask Him for His forgiveness. It will become evidently clear that our hearts are clean before God, and it will free our conscience to pray in confidence.

There is a vast amount of issues to pray about, both in our personal lives and for others. As you begin to pray the spirit of the Lord will bring to mind the things that you ought to be praying about. Sometimes, it maybe about a particular person, or a situation in your own life that needs God's intervention, but whatever it is, let us be attentive to what the Spirit is saying. Other times it maybe that our heart has developed sin and it needs to be exposed to the blood of Jesus.

We should be aware and quick to deal with all known sin in our own lives, immediately. Sometimes we can't wait to spread the failures of others. It is a wise thing to take the beam out of our own eye, rather than trying to remove the mote in our brother's eye. If we think of a beam it is much larger than a mote, wouldn't you agree? So let's be wise and do the honest thing by assessing our own failures and ask for forgiveness.

There is no one that can say that they are completely perfect and without sin or failures. We are all striving to get it right, so let us help each other that no one may fall by the way. The more we pray for one another the more we grow to love each another.

We are commanded to pray for all men in general and particularly for men in authority. They are in constant need of our prayers for they have many difficulties that they encounter. There are so many snares to which their duty has exposed them. We are to pray for one another, for ourselves, our families, and for people all over the world. Although it might be a large area, but we must pray for all men everywhere, for those who may have requested our prayers and just as importantly, for our enemies.

We should let our requests be made known to God with a heart of thanksgiving. We can count it a privilege to pray in Jesus name to God for everything and about everything; although He already knows it is our bound duty to tell Him. What a great relief it is when we can go to our Father and expose our heart to Him, it is joyous; it gives a feeling of gratitude to be free from the heavy burden.

How Should We Pray?

First and foremost we should pray in faith, and for the increase of our faith, with humility. This will increase our confidence to believe that whatsoever we pray about, God will hear and He will answer. We could use the method of the Lord's Prayer; it is a good example. As we continue to pray we will experience how to pray, and develop depth in our prayers. Sometimes prayer is simple and shallow, but at other times we may find ourselves engaged in warfare prayer. Other times it may seem that the more we pray, the more there is a need for prayer. No wonder the word of God commands us 'to pray without ceasing'.

It does not matter so much how or where we pray, what really matters in our asking is repentance and asking forgiveness of all known sins to get rid of any blockage that would hinder our prayers. It is wise to make a clearance before we begin to pray; that means get it right with God and, where possible, men.

Our heavenly Father is willing to forgive us our sins if we ask Him. If we ask for forgiveness on a daily basis then we can be sure that our hearts are clean without any hindrances to our prayers. We are warned not to be like the hypocrites, who love to pray in public places where they can be seen, and how well they can pray, for they have their reward. We must pray in humility, and never with a proud heart, because God sees the proud afar off. He will not answer prayers from a heart that is not humble before Him.

Praying Position

Personally I like the position of kneeling when praying, but, for those with painful knees, you can choose a position that is comfortable. Prayer is more than just a 'Hello, good morning Jesus'. That is not a good attitude to take. We must put some effort into our prayers, because when the real problems of life get hot and severe, the only solution is to get down to reality in prayer. So be prepared to position yourself for warfare, which can last more time as the Spirit enables. It is the Spirit that helps us pray for we do not always know what to pray about, but He helps our infirmities with 'groanings that cannot be uttered'.

Saying all this, it does not really matter what position we choose to be in when we pray. We can pray standing, kneeling, sitting, walking, lying down on our faces, or in whatever other position that suits us best. The position we decide to be in when we pray is not really important to God. It is what is in the heart, and the relationship that we have with the Father that matters. One of the benefits in prayer is the right to call God 'Abba', an affectionate term meaning 'Father'. This marvelous relationship carries responsibilities with it, as well as privileges.

These are some example of men's prayer positions:

NEHEMIAH used a standing position in prayer, see chapter 9:5.

PAUL bowed his knees when he prayed, see Ephesians 3:14.

EZRA 9:5 states that in the evening sacrifice he arose from fasting, and tore his garment, and his robe, he fell on his knees and spread out his hands to the Lord, and prayed.

JESUS entered the Garden of Gethsemane and fell on His knees and prayed until His sweat became like drops of blood.

What position do you use when you pray?

We cannot demand favors from God in tones of aggression, but we can be as partners, and as workers together with Him. God said His word will go out of His mouth, and it shall not return to Him void, but it shall accomplish that which He pleases, and it shall prosper in the thing where He sends it. *What an assurance!*

The Lord's Prayer

The first phase of the Lord's Prayer establishes the essential attitude for efficacious praying. The Old Testament prophets did acknowledge God as Father of the nation of Israel, and as the Fatherhood of all creation who operates in the life of every individual. Jesus told His disciples that He speaks to God intimately as a father. He is our Father and we are His children, we have a right to pray 'Our Father' (Matthew 6:9-13).

The first three parts of this prayer relates to God, and His honor, and the latter three are petitions, they are for our concern. The method of this prayer directs us to first seek the kingdom of God and His righteousness and then all other things shall be added.

Our Father

The Father is the first person of the Trinity. Scripture identifies the Fatherhood of God in five areas. He is the Father of creation (James 1:17); He is the Father of Israel (Jeremiah 31:9); He is the unique Father of Jesus Christ. He is a protective Father, emphasizing His defense of the poor and oppressed (Psalm 68:5). He is the Father of redemption when we become the children of God (John 1:13 and Romans 8:15). Just as an earthly father provides many benefits for their children, so our heavenly Father provides a number of spiritual benefits. To enjoy such benefit from God our spiritual Father we must be born again and become sons and daughters of God (John 1:12).

'Our Father who is in heaven' indicates that God is not only holy, but also He is personal and loving. We will notice that the first line of this prayer was a statement of praise and a commitment to hallow, or honor, God's holy name. Jehovah is His name. His name should never be used lightly, because God is holy. He deserves to be reverenced by all.

Hallowed Be Thy Name

The verse addresses the attention of the prayer towards God, and reverence for His name and His person. We must give glory to God before we can expect to receive mercies and grace from Him. We let Him have the praise of His perfections and allow ourselves to have the benefits of them. In prayer our thoughts and affections are to be carried out to the glory of God. We desire and pray that the name of

God, that is God Himself, maybe sanctified and glorified in us. The 'throne room' of God is our sanctuary, so divinely called the throne of grace. He bids 'Come boldly' to the throne of grace where we will find strength for the time of need.

Thy Kingdom Come

This refers to the eschatological nature of this prayer; the Kingdom is to be prayed for, implying that it has not yet fully arrived. The Kingdom represents the full and effective reign of God, through the mediatorial office of the Messiah.

with intensity, earnestly awaiting His Kingdom to be fully realized.

This petition has a reference in the doctrine that Christ preached: the Kingdom of Heaven is at hand. It is very significant that we pray the word when communicating with our Father. Thy Kingdom come is expressing the longing for a society on earth where God's will be done perfectly as in heaven.

We pray that the Kingdom of God comes, so that others and ourselves may be brought into obedience to all the laws and ordinances of it.

Thy Will Be Done

This emphasizes the idea that prayer is to bring about the conformity of the will of the believer to the will of God. Therefore prayer is an act of spiritual expression that brings us into conformity to the very nature and purpose of God.

We are asking God to use us as individuals. When we pray we are saying, 'Lord, enable me to do what is pleasing to thee, give me the grace that is necessary to do right and have the knowledge of what is thy will.'

We must realize that it is through the knowledge of God that we know His will in our prayer. We must also realize when we pray, that if our request is to be granted, it must please God.

This is the confidence that we have toward God that if we ask anything in His name He hears us and will grant us according to His divine will (1John 5:4). Our duty is to approach the throne of grace with boldness and believe that He hears us.

He whispers so we may find grace in the time of need. We are welcome to stay in His presence; there is no hurry or having to line up to be answered. He is waiting, call today.

Thine is the kingdom: God gives and saves like a king for God owns everything. Thine is the power, which is needed to maintain and support that Kingdom in the pattern of The Lord's Prayer. It all belongs to our God.

Give Us This Day Our Daily Bread

The petition begins with 'Give us this day our daily bread', which could apply to the provision of food in general. The term 'daily' fits in the Old Testament example of daily provision of manna to the Israelites while they were wandering in the wilderness (see Exodus 6:14:15).

We pray for the necessary support and comfort in this present life. There is a lesson to be learned in every word here. We ask for bread, not dainties, but that which is wholesome. We ask for our bread that teaches us honesty and industry. Because our natural being is necessary to our spiritual being in this world, therefore we should strive for the things of God's glory, Kingdom and will.

We ask for our daily bread that teaches us not to take thought of tomorrow, but constantly depend on divine providence. We beg of God to give it to us. The greatest of men must look to the mercy of God for this daily bread. Jesus emphasized that He is the Bread of life; anyone who eats of this bread will never be hungry again. So it is also spiritual bread that satisfies body, soul, and spirit. If our sins are not pardoned, this means that we should pray for daily pardon, just as we pray for daily bread.

We pray, 'Give us this day, not for me only, but for others in common to me'. This teaches us charity and a compassionate concern for the poor and needy. Give us this day shows the desire of the souls towards God and the wants of our bodies are renewed.

We need the daily bread that our heavenly Father supplies. Just as we could not live daily without food, so we cannot live daily without prayer. There must be a connection to the giver of life, to enable continuing breathing. This daily bread is available to those who are hungry for the word of God. He will also provide us with the natural bread that satisfies the human hunger.

There are guidelines on how to access this bread in the scriptures. *Have you come across them?* Jesus said, 'I am the Bread of life; if any man eat of this Bread he will live forever.' (John 6:51.) For the believers in Christ, bread may represent the Bible, Jesus, Christian fellowship, or any of the provisions God has made to supply our spiritual needs.

Forgive Us As We Forgive Our Debtors

This refers to sins, which are moral and spiritual debts to God's righteousness. The request for forgiveness of sin is made here by the believer. In order to be pardoned one needs not name all the sins individually, but must confess that he is a sinner.

God's forgiveness is rooted in His own deity and power. He alone has the power to forgive man His sins. We must recognize that everyone who sends a prayer heavenward stands in need of forgiveness; the repentance of the sinner does not produce forgiveness. God's forgiveness stems from His heart and will. Therefore, a person has no right to hold grudges against another.

As the Lord forgives us so we should be willing to do likewise to others. As we forgive others our heavenly Father will also forgive us. Forgiveness requires us to deal with the very people that we need forgiveness from, or who we must forgive. God will bring people together who need to forgive each other. One should take the opportunity and do the right thing while time is available. As we forgive our debtors, we are made perfectly new.

For example, consider the story of Joseph and his brothers who intended to do him evil, but God meant it for good. We can understand that Joseph had every reason to be bitter and hold his brothers in his heart for doing him wrong, but he chose to suffer rather than to hold malice even though it was painful (Gen 50:20).

The relationship between Joseph and his brothers was soon restored. God made it possible for Joseph and his brothers to forgive each other although his brothers rejected, kidnapped, enslaved, and imprisoned him. They were unfaithful and showed revenge, spite, and jealousy towards him. Nevertheless he graciously forgave them and shared his prosperity with them. Joseph demonstrates how God forgave us, and how He has showered us with His goodness, even though we have sinned against Him.

The beauty of this story is that Joseph was not overwhelmingly bitter. He did not take revenge upon his brothers. Joseph's care for his brothers is a remarkable story of forgiveness. It came to the time when circumstances changed and left the evil brothers at the mercy of Joseph. He provided such love for them even after they had dealt badly with him. This same forgiveness and fellowship can be ours if we ask for them.

Unforgiveness Can Harm

Results from a study was reported of a group of doctors who were asked to name the emotions that people suffer from that are responsible for physical illness. Their reply was anger and unforgiveness. Research shows that if these two deadly weapons are allowed to remain in our hearts they will cause toxins in the body and have a deadly effect on our emotions and wellbeing. This toxin will do an enormous damage in behavior patterns and other areas of our personality. It will make it impossible to get along with friends, families and people who we come in contact with. We will find that people will avoid us and be hesitant to join our company. Sometimes people will not be honest about our behavior towards them, they will just avoid having anything to do with us. Let us take some time to do an evaluation on our own selves, and then we will be able to understand the action and reaction of others.

An unforgiving behavior is the root of all bitterness and should not be allowed to live comfortably within the believer's heart. We can truly say that none of us is perfect, but we can still try toward perfection. We must be open to ourselves and go to God for help to deal with this deadly sin; He has the antidote to get rid of this… before it becomes rooted in our emotions. Be reminded that we have redemption through His blood, even the forgiveness of sins (Colossians 1:14).

The spirit of unforgiveness is a terrible sin that should be dealt with immediately, otherwise the individual will experience the effect of it in their memories. If an old hurt is brought up all the time the hurt will get deeper until it becomes a way of life. Remember that there is nothing so bitter that God's grace and forgiveness cannot root out, but we must be willing to let them go. If resentment, anger or hurt is allowed to fester the individual can suffer both spiritually and physically. The damage can be fatal. This is one reason why forgiveness is so important to remedy situations when they arise, and to move us on in full fellowship again. Ephesians 4:26 teaches us not to allow the sun to go down on our wrath.

Colossians 3:13 states that we should be willing to forgive whatever grievance we have against one another even as the Lord forgave us. This has proven to be a healthy action and good remedy for the soul and mind. We must forgive and forget the wrongs done; it will be proven in freedom of spirit and joy from within. This is a moral qualification for pardon and peace, which encourages hope that God will forgive us also. It will be evidence that 'He hath forgiven us having wrought in us the condition of forgiveness'.

Lead Us Not Into Temptation

God does not lead us into temptation, but allows us to be tested by them. God is not responsible for man's temptation to sin, yet we are invited to ask Him to help and to provide a way of escape, to build a hedge around us like He did for Job *(Job 1: 10).*

This is a plea for the providential help of God in the daily confrontation with the temptation of sin. God does not tempt us to do evil; we are tempted by our own lusts according to James 1:13. God allows us to be tested in order to give us the opportunity to prove our faithfulness to Him.

Having prayed that the guilt of sin might be removed we must pray as it is fitting, that we may never return to folly again. We pray that we will be delivered from evil, from the evil one, the devil, the tempter. We should keep under the watchful eyes of our Father that we might not be overcome by temptation or by evil. Sin is the worst of these evils, the evil that God hates, and which Satan tempts men with, and destroys them by.

Deliver Us From All Evil

To be delivered from evil we must to be constantly fighting the battle against this evil; we need the grace of God to remain eligible. As Christians we should pray to be delivered from these trying times and for deliverance from Satan (the evil one) and his deceit. Although we all struggle with temptation, sometimes it is so subtle that we don't even realize what is happening to us, but God has promised that He will not allow us to be tempted beyond what we can bear. We can ask God to help us recognize temptation and give us strength to overcome, and choose God's way instead.

Our sins are our debts, and there is a debt of duty that as creatures we owe to our Creator. We do not pray to be discharged from this, but upon the non-payment of this is a debt of punishment. Our daily duty is to forgive our debtors. If we forgive others who have done us wrong, our heavenly Father will forgive us when we have done wrong also.

Life is a give and take situation. Just as how we would like to be treated, we should do likewise and treat others fairly and with respect. In other words don't issue out to others that which you do not wish to receive yourself. If we pray in anger we have reasons to fear that God will answer in anger. It has been said, 'Prayers that are made in wrath will write in gall'. But man's passion shall not frustrate God's word. God's word will frustrate man to turn from sin to repentance.

Thine Is The Kingdom, The Power And The Glory

God is all in all; our prayers should be in a form of praise and thanksgiving. We praise God and give Him glory not because He desires our praises, because He is praised by a world of angels, and so man has an obligation to give God praise. He deserves to be praised for His excellent greatness. Praise Him for the work of redemption, the happiness of heaven, and all who are destined for heaven must begin to praise God now. We praise God because He grants us forgiveness so we can be free from the burden of sins. We praise God for His invitation to come boldly to the throne of grace where we will find grace to help us in the time of need.

God knows us better than we know ourselves; our lives are as an open book before him. He provides reproof, correction and instruction. God our Father deals with us as His sons and daughters. He often has to chastise us through His word to keep us in line so that we may be complete in Him. We should take God's chastisement with joy even though no correction is sweet at the time it is given, but when the result comes we can give God thanks for the end result. The best pleas in prayer are those that are taken from God Himself, and from that which He had made known of Himself. We must wrestle with God in His own strength to rid ourselves from this sin of unforgiveness.

In His promise we are invited to come boldly to the throne of Grace. The scriptures tell us to draw near to God and He will draw near to us. Many people desire to have the good things from God, to know the truth, and to find out His purpose, but they sometimes find it difficult to go through the process. It is necessary to have clean hands, a pure heart and to draw near to God through living a life of prayer, commitment, devotion and persistency.

Believers have often experienced and faced difficult situations, but great experiences can be gained through prayer in those trying times. We must make up our minds to stay the course, until we are consumed with the presence of Almighty God; prayer unlocks faith in our lives so the impossible can be seen as possible.

Effective prayer needs to be both an attitude of complete dependence on God and also an action in asking and believing. Prayer demonstrates our reliance on God as we humbly invite Him to fill us with faith and power to overcome. Therefore there is no substitute for prayer, especially in circumstances that seem to be impossible.

Sometimes we act as though the word *can't* impact the change we ask for. We fail to believe in our all-sufficient God, who created all things. Come on, readers, trust in your faith in Jesus to fix that problem that holds you in captivity as you ask in the name of Jesus; ask, believe and let it go. There is a blessed hour of prayer, your duty is to make that hour of prayer available and use it to the glory of God. There are days we can be all alone with Christ our Lord; there we can tell Him of our troubles alone. He will give us quick relief; let's take time out to tell him.

God's 'Amen'

Amen is like the signature of the prayer, the sealing and signing off of our requests. But more importantly, 'Amen' assures us that it is granted, it shall be so. Amen is a summary of what is desired, declaring *let it be so* as we have asked. It is a token of our desires and assurance to be heard that we say Amen. It is as though we say, 'I rest my case in you, O Lord, my God.'

A man's hope of receiving an answer to his petition would rest entirely in the grace of God. Amen.

Join me in prayer.

Holy righteous Father, I come to thee in the name of Jesus Christ Your exalted Son. Father I give You praise, honor and glory. Father You are great! There is none like You Lord; truly we have seen Your handiwork, the heaven so wonderfully displayed. Oh Father, we laud You for Your attributes, how excellent is Your name in all the earth.

Father, I thank You for forgiveness, and of cleansing my sins. Thank You for the blood of Jesus Your beloved Son, who died to take away my sins, and the sins of others. Father I give You all the praises that is due to Your worthy name.

Lord, I bless Your name, I ask You in Jesus' name to ever keep Your hand upon my life so that I will never depart from Your truth. Teach me to love You with my whole heart and my fellowman also.

Grant me understanding that I may know how to walk by Your word. Father, as I seek to develop a life of prayer, so I ask You to open my eyes of understanding that I may understand Your will for my life.

I ask this in Jesus' name.

Amen

2

Author's Testimony

Blessed are they who hunger and thirst after righteousness, for they shall be filled. Matthew 5:6

After I read the account in Matthew 9:11, on how Jesus' followers were so anxious in learning how to pray, I too had the same interest and set out to search for useful methods of effectively prayer. It took me years to develop the art of praying and I am still in the process of learning. On this delicate subject, one would never tire of exercising one's faith. During this time I had a deep yearning to get it right with God.

One morning I was praying and confessing my sins, my disappointments, my regrets, my pain, my shame, and all else I could think about that was preventing me from receiving the blessing. Suddenly, a word dropped into my spirit: *'You have not yet passed repair'*. I thought about the words and began to analyze their meaning.

I thought about when something is smashed or broken beyond recognition.

As I pondered, however, I thought to myself that if God said so, He is able to do the repair. I give thanks to God, that He had considered me; He has me on His mind, and cares what happens to me.

Considering my prayer at the time of receiving this, I thought this was really awesome. I felt a release in my sprit. I thought, 'O yes, I'm still on the Potter's wheel for repairing'. The Potter wants to put me back together again. He is still working on me... and it's the same for you. That means that I don't have to stay the way I am, He can work on my personality, my emotions, my desires, my fears and worries, He can make me into someone beautiful... I don't know about you but sometimes I do feel tired of the way I am. I have tried to get it right and I failed miserably. I am not one for staying down, I am always willing to get up and brush myself off and try again. I can understand when the apostle Paul cried out, 'O wretched man that I am; who shall deliver me from this body of sin'. There is always a fight for the right. We all feel that fight.

I realized that there were more challenges that I needed to deal with. Because life is constantly moving, one has to keep on seeking God's wisdom to know how to deal with situations as they present themselves, whether we are up to it or not. I relied solely on prayer and reading and meditating on the word of God as my guidance. When I read about the potter's wheel, in Jeremiah 18, I visualized myself on that wheel, as the potter is kneading *me*... as He did to the clay. At one point the vessel was marred in the potter's hand; he could have thrown the clay away, but he made it into another vessel.

I rejoice greatly, for although the vessel (myself) was marred in the potter's hand he saw it possible to remake it into another vessel. *Wonderful Jesus!* I am still on the Potter's wheel for my sanctification, which is a constant cleansing. It is a progressive work of the Holy Spirit.

I did not realize that my *all* must be on the altar of sacrifice, slain. All must be under the Spirit's control because I can only be blessed and have peace and sweet rest as I give Him my body and soul. I burst out in tears and praises, in gratitude to God for bringing me to the place of fully surrendering my life to Him

'Hallelujah to Jesus', as from that time of my confession and consecration I began to seek the face of the Lord more regularly through prayer and meditation on the word of God. My prayer life started to improve for the better. I took a special interest in reading books, the Bible, magazines, and to sow more intensely in prayer. It was then that I developed a burning desire to write a book to share with others *effectiveness in prayer*. I thought that every one could read and understand more about this topic, and be a part of this inspiring subject.

This has been a bumpy ride. Because the subject is prayer, I began to experience attacks from within and without. I was never a laid back person by personality, I am one who likes to get up and go, but I just could not get started. I would jot down words on a few pages but it would just not get ahead. My interest would be on other things to write about apart from the subject that was burning within me. I began to write a lot of inspirational pieces and send them to people as encouragement, but all these still did not fulfill my dreams to write a book on effective prayer. (You will find extracts of those writings sent out in the back of this book.)

I made a decision that I would double up my prayer time and go all out in prayer. Slowly, all my 'Why's' turned into 'Yes Lords'. I felt God's purpose, inspiration, and divine favor on my life. I began my journey by praying for myself, my children, families, friends, and for the needs of others more intensely. I turned those moments to 'prayer moments'. I thought, 'This is it. This is my time to write about the long awaited guide to effective prayer'. Because I had so many experiences through prayer, when I finally began to write this book the information would flow through, it was already there in my subconscious. I did not have to feel for information or surf the net on the subject of prayer because it was already in my daily agenda.

I decide to convert one of the rooms in my house into a Prayer Room, where I could spend quality time with the Lord in prayer. Each morning, and sometimes in the afternoon or at night, when I feel the moments to worship, I know it's time to go to the Prayer Room for a quiet moment with my Father. I tell you, the Holy Spirit will give you a loving reminder, an urge that it's prayer time. I truly believe that prayer will open closed doors, take you before kings and before people of influence.

Prayer will allow good people to come into your life. You will be exposed to other praying people and groups together; everyone will experience the benefit of staying the course through prayer. Praise God!

I once had a dream about going to see the Duke of Edinburgh. The Duke was the husband of the reigning Queen of England. It was so exciting that when I woke up I regretted the fact that it was just a dream, but I am waiting in anticipation to see, and meet, and greet the King of Glory. That will be a meeting and a half, *no, let's say a meeting in full.* So I am doing my best each day, taking time in prayer, developing, reading God's word and looking after my fellowman. It is said that love is better shown than to say, 'I love you'. In other words, 'Show me your love'.

God will lead you into the path of righteousness. His rod and His staff will provide comfort in the wailing storms of life. It will not be all plain sailing but with Jesus on board you can rest in the eye of the storm. My assurance in the storm will be with my hands lifted up and my heart aglow to know that the Master of every condition is interested in me… and you.

As I progress in my Christian journey, it just gets better every day. I see the need to develop a closer and personal relationship with God. Through a life of prayer I realize that it can be made possible if I ask the Lord to increase my faith and remain persistent with a strong determination to succeed. It has been a tough task but I believe that I can do all things through Christ who strengthens me, according to

Philippians 4:13, and so I am still in the process of learning how to pray effectively.

I'm still on the Potter's wheel. The wheel is still moving around getting rid of all my sins and shortcomings, because they were so many. They were higher than Mount Everest but through the blood of Jesus I watched the mountain slide down without human hands. *Praise God… thank you Jesus.*

Applying myself to prayer has helped me to become more mature as a Christian. Some of the things that used to be burdensome to me have become small; my life has changed dramatically. It allows me to think twice or otherwise before giving an answer when a situation arises. There is now a delay in my reactions and actions as if to say, 'Wait, don't answer so quickly. Think about it, pray about it; pray about everything. Hear what the Spirit is saying.'

I have now developed a passion to share and give encouraging words to others. When I see someone who is hurting, or maybe facing a crisis, a sense of compassion sweeps over me to help in whatever way possible. I see the need to assist in giving a loving word, or sharing on a word from the Bible that will give a lift in their spirit, a word that will take the pressure off, and a word that will help to lift their faith, and tell the devil to get lost. I have experienced real hurt in my personal life; this has given me the compassion to reach out to others in a very special way.

hand of God in many ways, saying, 'Don't be afraid, I'm here, I will never leave you or forsake you. You can make it even on broken pieces.' I tell you after hearing these words of reassurance, no matter how low you've been, you can lift up your head and give God thanks. I believe that God must have seen something in me far more than what others or I myself could see. Yes, He looked beyond all my faults and saw my needs. He had a plan for my life, a beautiful plan to be carried out by only *me*. He has chosen me to do so… *It is good that He has chosen me… how about you?*

This is one of my reasons for reminding people to pray in faith, and when things don't work out according as one would expect, it is good to go back to God and ask Him to increase our faith. Faith to rise again, to walk again, to love again, to sing again, to praise again, no matter how things seem difficult. God is all-sufficient, all-powerful, full of forgiveness, and plenteous in mercy. He can handle any hardcore, deep-rooted, impossible case; every one of them is simple in His hands. Our duty is to bring them all to Jesus. Even at the crossroad of life, there is life for the caller… God is at the other end of the line; all you need do is call.

There are times when you call a friend and you might get a busy signal, or you might be asked to leave a message, but heaven's telephone line is open and always available. We can get in touch with Him night or day. I have gained an understanding of what it means by 'keeping the fire on my secret altars' burning; the family altars will light their fire from the flames. We must keep that fire alight because so many of God's people have allowed their fire of love to burn so low that it is only the ashes that remain.

Secret devotions are the very essence, the evidence and barometer of vital and experimental religion. There can be no substitute for closet session; it has to be regular and frequent and free from disturbances. I have also discovered that a well-balanced prayer life will be enhanced richly by using the elements that are suggested. I should adore Him, worship Him, praise Him, give Him glory, and He will listen to His children with an open heart.

My friend, believe me that God is interested to hear from His children when they pray in faith. We must seek to demonstrate the elements of praise, adoration, thanksgiving, and worship in our prayers. When all these are coupled with the anointing of the Holy Spirit, you will experience newness in your spiritual life. It did not take a long time to realize that a life of prayer is not one to cease; it is a constant daily work. The Holy Spirit reminds me when it's time to talk to the Lord, time to enter the quiet room, or wherever I can be alone with my Father in prayer. As I commit myself to prayer, certain times of day or at night, I would sense a strong urge to be alone with God. Then I would think, 'Wait a minute, this must be the Holy Spirit spurring me with an inner urgency to pray.' We must realize that if we are to develop effective prayer it will take time to train ourselves, to wait and listen to the voice of God. To gain God's attention takes time and commitment, and obedience; it just doesn't happen in a short moment.

The word of God is so strong that when the weakest person gets on their knees the devil trembles. I pray that he will not only tremble, but he will run in terror. On your knees, that is where it all begins, on your knees; when trouble hits I talk to Jesus right down on my knees. I tell you, it will develop into a determination that no matter what, you will pray. We are encouraged pray when it seems like nothing is shifting, nothing is happening, the condition, or person you have been praying about for many years remains the same. Take heart and continue; God is always true to His word, He will come through.

I tell you the truth, it is by faith and not what you see, because the underlying enemy works against our prayer all the time so don't be too quick to blame others; see the works of the evil one, and get wise. We are not blinded by what the enemy is doing, he has to do what he has to do, but we can be assured that God is still in control. You may even desire to 'feel' something when you pray, but it is by faith in Jesus. We must believe that Jesus is the Son of God and that He died for the remission of our sins.

We must carry on. As one of my daughters said, some of the things I am praying about might not happen until long after I am gone to be with the Lord. I totally agree with her but my duty is to continue praying to the Almighty God who hears prayers. Jesus has something to say about virtue in prayer. When the woman with the issue of blood touched Jesus He quickly recognized that someone had touched him, because He felt that virtue had left him...

Power had left Him. Do you need some of that power today? It is still available.

So, as I continue this exciting lonesome path in prayer, it gets more interesting every day. We can pray our way out of every condition that seems impossible, because God is a God who specializes in the things that seems impossible with men.

Friends and loved ones have often asked to be remembered whenever I pray. Some have even sent photographs of their children to be prayed for from as far as over seas... Praise the Lord, for He is good and His mercies endures forever... I will bless the Lord at all times and His praises shall forever be in my mouth. Oh, taste and see that the Lord is good, blessed is the man that puts His trust in Him.

I give God thanks for His grace and mercy and for enabling me to keep learning about effective prayer, prayer that makes a difference, prayer that makes a shift into the presence of Almighty God.

Join me in prayer.

Our God and our Father I come to You through the exalted name of Your Son Jesus Christ. I want to take this opportunity to thank You for a life of prayer.

Father, we thank You for the love and concern that You have constantly showed to Your people. Truly Lord, I have come so far by faith leaning on Your promises. I realize that it could have only been through the death of

Your Son Jesus that I could have remissions of sins. I thank You.

Father, thank You for deliverance, healing, comfort, peace and tranquility in my inner most being. Lord, I bless Your holy name. O the riches of Your grace, they are past finding out. Father, I honor Your holy name.

And so, Father I ask in Jesus' mighty name to keep me near the cross where the fountain is still flowing, that I may not wander in the path of sin as long as I should live, but be constantly looking to Your sustenance as my source.

I also ask that You will bless Your people that are near and far, and increase a longing in them for more of thee, that they will always have a desire to seek the things that are eternal.

I give You praise, and thank You again as I ask these mercies in Jesus Christ's name.

Amen.

3

Kinds Of Prayers

Secret Prayer

Our Father is always willing to listen to the things we wish to confess to Him in secret prayer. He is a good secret-keeper. He will not tell anyone our secrets. We need not feel ashamed to approach Him in secret, just 'Him and I.' Christ is our mediator, because His death satisfied the wrath of God against sin and paid the death penalty for our sins. If we confess our sins to God, He is faithful and just to forgive and to cleanse us from all unrighteousness. If we sin against God alone, then the confession needs to be to Him alone; to make confession to someone else would serve no purpose. We can whisper to our Father in secret because He reads our hearts. Even before we go to Him in prayer He knows what we are about to say, or ask (Matthew 6:8).

It is reassuring when confession to God is in secret. Although the sin that is committed might be grave, when talking to our heavenly Father we are confident that He hears and will answer our prayer. He is faithful and just to forgive and cleanse us from all unrighteousness. When I confess my sins to my Father in private, it is similar to having a private conversation with our boss, a minister of the gospel, a close friend, or someone who we really trust. In this kind of setting we can be open and feel free and comfortable to express ourselves without having to hold back.

Some sins that are committed are done against God. The general principle is that the confession should be coexistent with the sin. Confession should be made to the offended party as well as to God. The prodigal son's sin was against his father and against God. He made his confession and said, 'I have sinned against heaven and in your sight' (Luke 15; 21). Confessing our sins to God alone would have been inadequate and not brought peace of conscious restoration and relation to him and his father (Matthew 5:23-24).

The order is to first go and confess, then reconcile and present your gift. Once we have confessed and rejected sin, we can now begin a life of integrity. You may ask, 'How do I do this?' We can make frequent evaluations of where we are, assessing our attitude, behavior, and accomplishments.

The secret of the Lord is with them who fear Him, therefore there is no secret that is not open before our Father, nothing is hidden from

His eyes, and all things are open before Him. The darkness and the light are alike to Him.

The Psalmist says that even if we were to go to the bottom of the sea God is there (Psalm 139). If we should make our bed in hell, He is there. The light and the darkness are both alike; anywhere men find themselves God sees him. Our God never sleeps or slumbers. He is so great and our world is small to Him. He is not merely the God of the sun and the stars, but He is the God who is concerned with the smallest baby, with the most seemingly insignificant person, with the life and feelings of every person, no matter how young or old… we are His concern.

The more we think how undeserving we are it should be our interest to take time to worship him; this will help us to grow strong in body, soul, and spirit. Our life is as an open book to Him, nothing is covered, and nothing is hidden from His watchful eyes. When Adam sinned in the garden and he was hiding from God, he failed miserably. God knew where he was and what he had done.

Even when we pray in secret God sees our tears and commitment, He will reward us openly. When we spend time alone with God in prayer, scripture reading and worship we are moved in the right direction for a closer walk with God. In our secret we have the opportunity to find out what God will have us to do.

Secret prayer is very personal and sacred to the individual. No one else can pray that prayer that God wants you to personally lift up to him. Public prayers are necessary, but private, devotional prayer is spiritual and a good foundation. We can open up our hearts, our fears, our disappointments, and say all that would seem like an embarrassment in other settings. What a place to be, having a secret talk with our Father.

We are much familiar with the story of Daniel. Though he knew that the writing was signed against him he went into his house, with his windows opened towards Jerusalem, kneeled down on his knees, and prayed three times a day, giving thanks to God (Daniel 6:11-13).

Daniel did not rely on a habit that was not known to him; he was acquainted to personal, devotional prayers. The place where he prayed was already prepared, devoted and private, and demonstrates a position of kneeling. This position indicates his humility. The frequency of three times says a lot regarding his persistence, and he also gave thanks. Daniel exercised all the elements of prayer when he prayed. The closet is regarded as the secret place of prayer. It can be a quiet place where all distractions are excluded, only the heavenly Father's presence is important. The Lord does not specify the time, or place for such secret prayer. It is up to the individual to determine the times, morning, afternoon or at night, to pray.

With consistency, fervency, and commitment we can develop the discipline for a life of effective prayer. This is where a life of prayer will take us; it will lead us in the path of righteousness. There we will meet the King of glory. This is where only few are welcomed; it is in the throne-room. You will not be counted as a guest or a visitor but you will be treated as a child of the King. There is tremendous blessing in being alone with God. It is such a joy to be in His presence alone. We can talk to Him with openness in ways that we could hardly share with our earthly friends; we can express our love and weaknesses, our unrest and our concerns. What a privilege to be able to carry everything to God in prayer.

Readers, I just feel like going to God right now, will you join me in prayer? Let's pause to have a quiet moment with our Father.

Father, we glorify your excellent name, and we give You praise. We love You Lord, we lift up our hearts to You in prayer. Breathe on us Your children, as we give You thanks, in Jesus Christ's name. Amen.

How do you feel? I just experienced a sense of renewal for that short pause communing with our Father. However, it's not all about feeling; it is by faith in Jesus that we believe that He hears when we pray, we give Him thanks. We can commune in such a way to receive strength for greater service. I can testify that some of the richness that I have experienced is when I am alone with God.

The Holy Spirit is our helper. In times of perplexity and embarrassment, and strong temptation, the Holy Spirit will be present to help us pray. The Psalmist wrote, 'He who dwells in the secret chamber of prayers lives under the protection of the Almighty. I will say of the Lord He is my refuge and strength, a very present help in trouble. I will not fear though the earth be removed and is carried into the midst of the sea, God is there.'

It is advisable not to live partially in God's presence, or out of His presence, for the risk is too great. The enemy might try to get us and destroy us; and we might not be able to get back safely, therefore it is advisable to stay in the secret place of our Father.

A secret place is not exposed to everyone, especially our enemies. God's secret place is not free for all and it cannot be invaded easily. It is a place where only the righteous is invited. There is a great barrier, a two-edged sword, twenty-four, seven, as a shadow set between; it is too secure for thieves to break in. Praise the Lord.

At times we are prone to keep quiet about the blessings of God towards us. We often miss the opportunities to testify of the mercies of God; we miss opportunities to attest to His faithfulness. Admittedly, there is a time to be still, a time not to speak; but we must remember that there are many times when we should speak. Perhaps we have missed some golden opportunities, some choice times when a word from us about the goodness of God would have had a tremendous effect on a friend, an acquaintance, a visitor at church, a son, a daughter, or a parent. Let us make good use of every opportunity, as one proverb puts it, make hay while the sun is shinning. Some souls are gone yonder with vast testimonies of the goodness of God; they carry these experiences with them to a place where it will have no more use to them, all of their memory will perish thereafter potentials. Things could have been otherwise, rather than spending time on things that are unnecessary, let us use the opportunity to talk about the goodness of the Lord, to give thanks. Tell it every day. Show it. Let others hear from your lips that God is good.

How am I dealing with evil thoughts? Am I struggling over and over with the same pitfalls? How can others see Christ in me? These are some concerns that should come from within, questions that will probe and disturb our conscience. Someone suggested that having a good reputation is what others think about you, while character is what you really are. We need both of these graces to live victoriously. Doing our own assessment through prayer is strongly recommended, it should be a regular exercise to set goals to guide us on our Christian journey. Be reminded that it is in the secret place of the Most High that victories are won.

Family Prayers

Acts 10:2

God always has an interest in the family. When the family prays together this must make the heart of God glad.

The family continues to be the primary means through which God demonstrates His ultimate intentions for His creation. The family is the intended way in which individuals are to be nurtured. God loves when the family is consistent in devotions, when all the family meets together and draws on strength from the word of God in Bible study.

The family is a viable part of God's order in the world.

Each member of the family has a part to play and will be helped to take up this role as early as possible as the parent seeks God's wisdom and leads them to the Lord. God's word says, 'And thou shall teach them diligently to thy children, and thou shall talk of them when thou sit in thy house, and when thou walk by the way, and when thou lie down, and when thou wake up' (Deuteronomy 6:7).

One thing that set Israel apart from all nations in early history was its strong emphasis on the family unit. The law was given to the heads of families with the commandment that they teach it to their children. It was enough for the father to remember the word of the Lord, but he was to teach them diligently to his children. It emphasizes the continuous process of discussing the word of God and applying it to an individual's life. The word of the Lord was to be taught and discussed as the family sat together in the house, when they walk along the way, when they lay down to rest, and when they rose up for a new day.

We read in Acts 10:2 that Cornelius was a devoted man who feared God. He was a man who also believed in family principles. He made sure that his household was aware of the importance of prayer. They joined in family worship and almsgiving generously to the people and prayed to God always. When a man takes the responsibility to order his household to love God and obey His commands this man is as a role model. Cornelius is a welcome example of God's willingness to use extraordinary means to reach those who desire to know Him. He does not play favorites and He does not hide from those who want to find Him. God sent His Son because He loves the whole world and that includes Peter, Cornelius, and you.

Cornelius was a Roman officer, a centurion and commander of a hundred soldiers. Although he was stationed in Caesarea, Cornelius would probably eventually return to Rome. Thus his conversion was a major stepping-stone for spreading the gospel to the empire's capital city. What will happen to the heathen who have never heard about Christ? This question is often asked about God's justice. Cornelius wasn't a believer in Christ, but he was seeking God and he was reverent and generous. Therefore God sent Peter to tell Cornelius about Christ. Cornelius is an example that God rewards those who earnestly seek Him.

Those who sincerely seek God will find Him. God made Cornelius' knowledge complete (Hebrews 11:6). God saw Cornelius was sincere in faith. His prayers and generous giving was a 'memorial offering before God', a sacrificial offering to the Lord. God answers the sincere prayers of those who seek Him by sending the right person or the right information at the right time.

Joshua said, 'as for me and my house, we will serve the Lord' (Joshua 24:15). Joshua publicly said that Israel is a free moral agent; each person has a right to choose their own God. God will not force anyone to serve Him. But Joshua made a commitment; his allegiance would be to serve his God. He made his choice to lead his family in devotion in truth in a strong biblical conviction, and to establish a right relationship to his God.

Praying In Groups

When two or more believers filled with the Holy Spirit pray sincerely according to God's will, and not their own, God will be pleased to grant them their requests.

Jesus looked ahead to a new day when He would be present with His followers, not in body, but through His Holy Spirit in the body of believers (the church). The sincere agreement of two people is more powerful than the superficial agreement of thousands, because Christ's Holy Spirit is with them.

Praying in groups gives a sense of togetherness. The Bible says in Matthew 18:20 that when two or three people are gathered together in God's name He will be there in our midst. It makes a stronger army of the Lord when we come together for prayer. When each person is calling on the Father, we know and are assured that He hears each prayer of everyone at the same time, without getting confused. Even before we call He promises that He will answer.

Praying collectively is a mighty force against the enemy. When the church meets to pray in prayer meeting, it gives support and strength to each other for the coming week. It is a setting that is useful in many ways. We get to know each other. People feel valued, and can't wait for the next meeting.

Believers in the early church were accustomed to house prayer. They often gathered in homes to pray and seek the face of the Lord. They went from house to house breaking bread. In many places this is still practiced by believers. For various reasons it is an effective method to win the family to Christ. Families who have very young children, and find it impossible to take them to church, may welcome this idea of hearing the gospel in the comfort of their own homes.

Praying In Public

When we pray in public we should not pray to impress the hearers, especially if one should be speaking in other tongues. The unbelievers would not understand what was being said. Speaking unintelligible langue is like piping or harping without distention of sounds: words without a meaning will not convene any motion, or instruction. See 1 Corinthians 11:4-14.

Some like to exercise this habit to show how well they can pray, and string empty words without giving God the praise. We have to be very careful that public prayers glorify God because He is the one we are supposed to be praying to. For if I pray in tongues, my spirit prays, but my understanding is unfruitful, what is the result? I will pray with my spirit, and I will also pray with my understanding, I will sing with my spirit and I will also sing with my understanding.

The Pharisees were noted for this practice of praying in public places where there were lots of people to hear them. It is not a bad thing, but it is the motive that they use so that others could hear how well they could pray. Jesus says in Matthew 6:5-6, 'and when thou pray, thou should not be as the hypocrites are for they love to pray standing in the synagogues and in the corners of the streets, that they maybe seen of men. Verily, I say unto you they have their reward. But when thou pray, enter into thy closet, and when thou have shut the door, pray to thy Father which is in secret: and Thy Father which sees in secret shall reward thee openly'.

Jesus was saying that those who pray to be heard by men have already received their reward, for having prayed so, they have been heard by men, and they were seeking to impress their hearers. He was not condemning public prayers, but He was warning us to be careful of our motives when we pray in public. Believers are expected to pray in public when are conducting and evangelizing street meetings, witnessing, or where ever duty calls for prayer. The believer must be ready to offer up prayer for those who ask. We are encouraged to pray for men everywhere, it is a command that cannot be missed or shirked. Not everyone has the ability to pray in public, but we can depend on the Holy Spirit who teaches men to pray. A good idea is to practice praying at home; this will enhance our confidence when we are asked to pray in public.

Join me in prayer.

Father who art in heaven, we hallow Your great name. How much we give You praise for the wisdom to know the difference between good and evil. Lord, I ask You please to give us wisdom to know how to pray in public places, so that whoever hears may have understanding of what is said. Truly Lord, You are good and Your mercies endure forever. One generation to another will come to experience Your goodness.

Father, You have said in Your word that they that put their trust in You shall be like Mount Zion that cannot be moved. Help me, O Lord, to trust You at all times, so that I will not be moved. Father, Your word also states that the just shall live by faith; Father increase my faith that I may live contentedly.

Lord, my soul has found rest in Your salvation. You alone are my rock and fortress. Lord, I believe that my faith will never be shaken, as long as I keep under the shadow of Your wings.

I ask You in the name of Jesus for a fresh experience of the joy of salvation in our lives. Father, help us to open our hearts to the truth of Your holy word. I ask that You would remember all those who are suffering from various illnesses, trouble, fear and anxiety, please help them to take their burdens to You, and put trust in You for their deliverance.

Father, help us to take You at Your word that says, 'By His stripes we were healed'. I pray for the manifestation of Your words in our lives, O Lord we groan to be near You.

Thank you, Lord, for Your blessings. I ask these mercies in Jesus Christ's name.

Amen

Parts Of Prayer

Adoration

Adoration is when we adore God, by honestly praising and appreciating Him for His holiness, and sovereignty. Adoration flows from a heart that is washed in the blood of Jesus, and has good fellowship and relationship with the Father. When King Nebuchadnezzar recovered from his distraction and returned to his right mind, he looked up as a penitent and humble petitioner for mercy. When he was restored to his kingdom he praised, extolled and honored the King of heaven (Daniel 4:37).

Here are a few examples of others who adored God:

DAVID regularly blessed the Lord in his prayers. He said, 'Thine, Oh Lord, is the greatest.' He placed a high emphasis on the Lord as a powerful warrior; he glorified the ornamental magnificence of God's works, declared that victory and possession of the earth belongs to Him. In the climax of his adoration he said, 'Thine is the kingdom'. David recognized that God is the source of all riches and honor, the ruler of all, and therefore offers thanks to God in humility (1 Chronicles 29:10-13).

THE WISE MEN came to worship Jesus. When they entered the house and saw the young child with Mary His mother, they fell down and worshiped Him. Then they opened their treasures and presented Him with gifts of gold, and of frankincense, and of myrrh (Matthew 2:1-11).

MARY'S life teaches us that although she was blessed and highly favored as the mother of Jesus it does not mean that all will be smooth sailing. Instead, her life shows that favor with God has an attachment of the willingness to suffer for the Lord.

THE LEPERS asked Jesus to cleanse them of their leprosy. They said, 'Lord, if you will you can make us clean.' Jesus put forth His hands and said, 'I am willing. Be thou clean.' After Jesus granted them their request He told them to go and show themselves to the priest. As they went they found that they were healed. When they saw that they were clean they worshiped God (Matthew 8:2).

THE RICH RULER was in authority but still saw the need to come to Jesus in an attitude of adoration. He said to Jesus, 'My daughter is near death. Come and lay your hands upon her and she will recover.'

THE DISCIPLES worshipped the Lord after they came out of the storm. After seeing Him calm that storm those who were in the boat worshiped Him saying, 'Truly you are the Son of God.' (Matthew 14: 22, 23)

THE BLIND MAN, realizing that he had received his sight, cried out and said, 'Lord, I believe.' He then worshipped Him (John 9:1-38).

THE GREEK WOMAN offered adoration to God. She came to Jesus and asked for mercy for her daughter who was grievously vexed with a devil. Jesus did not pay her attention, but that did not deter her; she was determined not to be denied. Despite her problem and His response to her request she cried 'Lord help me' and continued to worship Him. She was then granted her request (Matthew 15:22).

EVEN IN CREATION adoration is expressed. The scriptures declare that at the name of Jesus every knee shall bow, of those in heaven, and of those on earth, and those under the earth. Every tongue shall confess that Jesus Christ is Lord, to the glory of God the Father (Philippians 2:10-11).

What glorious examples and testimonies the scriptures show to help us understand how adoration and praise is essential in worshipping our God. It will engage us to minimize our problem and focus on the One who can save and deliver.

In contrast, **THE MOTHER OF ZEBEDEE'S SONS** came to Jesus with her two sons, kneeling down in worship. She asked a favor, that Jesus grant each of her sons a seat on His right and left in His kingdom. She gave Jesus worship, but her real motive was to selfishly get something from Him. Too often this happens in our churches and on our knees. We play righteous games, expecting God to give us something in return, but true worship, adoration and praise is an appreciation of Christ for who He is and what He has done (Matthew 20: 20-21).

Confession

The Greek word for confession means to 'admit or declare oneself guilty for what one is accused'. When we confess our sins to God, we are agreeing with Him in His judgment of our guilt and the seriousness of His consequence. We are viewing our sin from His perspective, in agreement with what He says is required of us. If our confession is not sincere and explicit it will not reach God's ear.

It is made clear in 1 John 1:9, that 'If we confess our sins He is faithful to forgive us our sins and cleanse us from all unrighteousness'. Confession of sin and a changed life are inseparable. Faith without deeds is dead, says James 2:14. This was Jesus' harshest words to the respectable religious leaders who lacked the desire of real change. They wanted to be known as religious authorities, but they did not want to change their hearts and minds, thus their lives were unproductive.

We should make confession of our sins the moment we are conscious of having sinned, and not delay until a more convenient time. We have the assurance that the moment we sincerely confess our sins, God freely forgives us and fellowship is restored.

A good example of confession in prayer can be found in the story of King Solomon just after he had finished building the house for God to dwell in. He prayed that God would own the house; that God would hear and accept the prayers that would be made toward that place. He asked that God would hear from His dwelling place, even from heaven, and that as He heard He would forgive. The forgiveness of sins makes way for the answers to our prayers.

King Solomon prayed that God would give judgment according to iniquity upon all the appeals that should be made to Him.

That God would return in mercy to His people when they repented and reformed and sought Him.

That God would welcome strangers to His house and answer their prayers. And that God would plead the cause of the people of Israel when they were oppressed and answer their prayers.

Solomon concluded his prayer by using words that he had learnt from his father David. He prayed that God would take possession of the temple and make it His resting place. That God would make His ministers of the temple a public blessing.

He prayed that God would clothe them with salvation, not only to save them, but to make them instrumental to save others. God heard the prayer of Solomon and immediately send down fire from heaven and consumed the sacrifice.

These are signs that God is pleased with the prayers that are prayed according to His will. God did the same to Elijah in 1 Kings 18:38 and in response to Gideon's prayer in Judges 5:21.

God was pleased with the sacrifice that was offered by David in 1 Chronicles 11:26. When the people saw what was done they worshipped and praised God. They bowed their faces to the ground and worshipped. They sensed their unworthiness in God's presence. Even when the fire of the Lord came down the people praised Him saying, 'He is good for His mercies endure forever'.

Public Confession

One should not be ashamed to confess Christ publicly. If we are ashamed to do so He will also be ashamed to own us before our Father who is in heaven.

Confession of our sins is supposed to free us to enjoy fellowship again with Christ. It should ease our conscience and lighten our care. Some people confess their sins over and over and refuse to accept that God sent His beloved Son to die so that He could offer us pardon. True confession involves a commitment never to continue in sin. We must constantly pray for strength to defeat temptation. If we are still feeling guilty we have the assurance in God's word that God forgives and forgets. He even stated that He will cast all our sins into the sea of forgetfulness. Since Jesus Christ advocates our defense, we cannot be tried for a crime for which we were already acquitted. Satan is the accuser who will try to bring back our past, but don't listen to his lies; he is a loser.

When the sin is done in public, against some group, or church, the confession should be done in public. In so doing the sin can be forgiven publicly, so that confidence can be restored and fellowship renewed, among all parties. This action sometimes will bring about a time of revival. One would have experienced an irresistible outpouring of the Holy Spirit that convicts the heart and causes us to confess our wrong doing to each other, resulting in forgiveness.

Contrition or penitence will accompany true confession. Deep contrition and penitence was seen in the confession of the prodigal son. He cried, 'I am no longer worthy to be called your son, make me one of your hired servants'. He confessed that he had sinned against his father, so he asked to be forgiven by his father (Luke 15:19). If an individual professes penitence without the intention to forsake the sin, it is insincere and a mockery.

There is another confession that we should regularly make: that Jesus Christ is Lord of our lives. With the heart man believes to righteousness, and with the mouth confession is made unto salvation (Romans 10:9; Matthew 10:32-33). As a daily habit we must continue confessing the goodness of God by reading, meditating on, believing, and praying the word of God.

We should make regular confession: 'I am a new creation'; 'I am born again'; 'I am a child of God'; and 'My sins are washed away in the blood of Jesus'.

Jesus promises that 'all who come to Him He will in no wise cast them out'. *Praise the Lord.*

Supplication

Supplication is asking God to supply our needs and the needs of others. It is a powerful source in the prayer ring. Supplication must be made to God in faith, believing. Various testimonies are recorded when a believer makes supplication to God for themselves and on behalf of others. They will always overcome victoriously.

Supplication is a humble request made to God by men in their prayers. The word of God tells us that we should make supplication on behalf of kings and all who live in the land, so that we may live peacefully (see 1Timothy 2:1-3).

Here are some examples of supplications made to God:

The Lord said to **KING SOLOMON,** 'I have heard thy prayers and thy supplications that thou hast made before me. I have hallowed this house which thou hast built, to put my name there forever; my heart and eyes shall be there perpetually' (1 King 9:3).

JOB prayed, 'though I were righteous, yet would I not answer, but I would make supplication to my Judge' (Job 9:15).

KING DAVID said, 'The Lord hath heard my supplication, and He will receive my prayer.' David knew the importance of making true confession, and how God heard and gave him the answers (Psalm 6:9).

HANNAH was barren and prayed that God would bless her with a child. She had a good reason to feel discouraged and bitter, because at that time someone else was sharing her husband and producing children. Nevertheless she prayed and sought the Lord. God heard her prayer and granted her request. With gratitude Hannah prayed and said, 'My heart rejoices in the Lord. In the Lord my horn is lifted high, my mouth boasts over my enemies, for I delight in your deliverance. There is no one holy like the Lord; there is no one besides you, there is no Rock like our God' (1 Samuel 2:10).

Although **THE GENTILE WOMAN** was a stranger to the Commonwealth of Israel, her request was answered because God has His people from all coasts and nations. God in His wisdom has chosen vessels from every tribe and nation, even in the most unlikely places. The woman cried to show her misery, she cried earnestly. She said: 'My daughter is grievously vexed with a devil'. The problems that affect children will also affect their parents. Parents will always feel the miseries of those who are their flesh and blood. It was the distress and trouble of this woman's daughter that brought her to Christ. She pleaded for mercy and came in faith, and He did not reject her. It is the duty of parents to be in earnest prayer for their children; we should bring them to Christ and believe that by faith and prayer He will hear and answer.

At first Christ did not answer the woman's cry; He turned a deaf ear that she might be more earnest in prayer. Likewise not every prayer is immediately answered. Sometimes God seems not to regard His people's prayers, but this is meant to increase our faith. Jesus' disciples wished that He would send the woman away because she was not of Israel. And Jesus told her that it was not right to take the children's bread and cast it to the dogs, which was how the Gentiles were looked upon by the Jews.

Hearing this, the woman sunk further down in despair, but there was a little truth in it that she should see herself only in God's mercy. Before we are fit to be dignified and have the privilege and be equal with God's chosen people, we should see ourselves as nothing before Him. Jesus will exercise our faith with great trials and He sometimes saves the sharpest for the last so that we may come forth as pure gold.

The woman could have thought, 'Why did I bother, why didn't I stay at home rather than come to hear Christ call me a dog?' She could have given up and stayed away from Christ forever, but she believed that Christ would have compassion on her.

She may not have fully understood the response of Christ with His great reputation for kindness, tenderness, and compassion but she overlooked this and pressed on.

Whatever discouragement she may have felt at first at Jesus' response the woman broke forth from all discouragement and worshipped Him saying: 'Lord help me.' She improved the intensity in her prayers, instead of blaming Christ or charging Him for ignoring her plea. She drew strength from just looking at the Master, knowing that He was indeed merciful. She humbled herself, worshipped Him, and cried again, 'Lord help me.' When the answers to prayers are deferred, God is teaching us to pray more.

The woman resolved that she had come for mercy and she would not let go without it being granted. Her prayers were short but had all the elements in it, in just those three words, 'Lord help me'. She finally agrees that she is unworthy and says, 'Truly Lord, even the dogs eat the crumbs that fall from the master's table. Truly Lord, I'm a dog and I have no right to the children's bread.' Then Jesus says, 'Oh woman, great is thy faith.' He commended her faith; He thought that the woman showed wisdom, humility, meekness, patience and perseverance in her prayers and all was the product of faith.

Daniel

Daniel prayed for his sins and the sins of the people of Israel. He said: *'O Lord, hear: O Lord, forgive, O Lord, hearken and do, defer not, for thine own sake, O my God, for thy city and thy people are called by thy name.'*

While Daniel was praying, and confessing his sins, and the sins of the people, He asked the Lord to turn away His anger and fury from His people.

Daniel based his prayer not in his own righteousness, but God's great mercies. While he was still praying God sends an immediate answer to Daniel's prayer of supplication.

An angel was sent swiftly to touch Daniel and reassure him that his prayer was heard. The angel called his name and said, 'O Daniel, I am come forth to give you skill and understanding.' God will answer our prayer in a variety of ways. To the person who dwells in the secret place of the most high, the Lord says, 'because he hast set his love upon him, therefore he will deliver him, I will set him on high, because he hath known my name, he shall call and I will answer him. I will be with him in trouble, I will deliver him and honor him; with long life will I satisfy him, and show him my salvation' (Psalm 91:14-16).

We are still dealing with the wonderful prayer tool of supplication; let us now look at how the apostle Paul focused on the need to pray with supplication.

Paul instructed the Ephesians to pray always with supplication in the spirit, watching with all perseverance for all saints. This should be made out of a sense of need making our requests known to God. Paul continues to encourage the saints to be careful for nothing, but in everything in prayer and supplication, with thanksgiving, let their request be made known unto God (Ephesians 4:6).

Paul instructs, 'Therefore first of all, that supplications and prayers, intercession and giving of thanks be made for men' (Ephesians 6:18).

Sometimes we wonder how to pray for missionaries and other leaders who we have not met. Paul had never met the Colossians, but he faithfully offers prayer for them. His prayer teaches how to pray for others, whether we know them or not. We can request that they understand God's will, and gain spiritual wisdom to please and honor God. He urges us to pray as he did for others, that God's strength, His great endurance and patience may be developed in them because all believers have these basic needs. The benefit that all believers have in Christ is that He made us qualified to share in His inheritance (2 Corinthians 2:21).

He also rescued us from Satan's dominion of darkness, and made us His children. He brought us into His eternal kingdom (Ephesians 1:5-6).

He redeemed and bought our freedom from sin and judgment (Hebrews 9:12), He forgave all our sins (Ephesians 1:7), so we give thanks for what we have received.

When we pray we should not feel that our prayers are in vain, because Christ can be touched with the feelings of our infirmities. He suffers with us through all our heartache and He is ready to do the best for us. At times in our struggle He is carrying us through the rough maze of life that we so often experience on the journey.

We too have the same opportunity to make supplication to God; He is just the same today as He was in years gone by. His ears are still open to His children's cry... let us cry out to God for His divine intervention. We cannot find the way without Him.

We are encouraged to continue in prayer. Sometimes the answer to our prayer may not be immediate, but we must exercise patience, for they that wait on the Lord shall renew their strength, and will mount up with wings as an eagle. Therefore prayer must be built up with perseverance. We may not always feel like praying, but until the answer comes, we might as well persevere; joy will come in the morning. We must be alert, and wait, as one who is anticipating the answer.

Sometimes it is so easy to talk about praying and making supplication, but with all good intentions, it takes consistence, determination, and discipline to live up to our talk about prayer. Nevertheless we must understand that amidst all that goes on against us, we must resist the temptation, break through every obstacle and find our knees in prayer. It is a helpful exercise to pray short prayers throughout the day as we offer praise and petition to God. It is a healthy practice to keep in touch with our Father who is in heaven. It might seem at times that heaven is a long way away but it takes just a 'call to connect you to the Father...' We will reap the benefit, if we continue our devotion to pray. We will experience that a life of prayer will also help us to witness to the unsaved effectively. This is a command from our Father to remind us and others of the grace and gift that He offers.

We are commanded to go and tell... It is called 'the Great Command' and in obeying that command the blessings of the Lord will overflow into the lives of others.

God deserves our best in worship, praise and respect. Sin has hardened our hearts to our true condition. Pride is unwarranted self-esteem; it is setting our own judgment above God, and looking down on others.

The hand that holds the occasion depth can hold my small affairs.

The hand that guides the universe can carry all my cares.

Regardless of how heavy the burden, how tangible the problems,

How serious the disease, the God of the galaxies has measureless, power to meet all our needs.

Petition

Petition means to beg or appeal, as in the instance of a beggar sitting at the wayside, asking for help from people who pass by. It expresses destitution and inadequacy, the inability to meet ones need; it is a need that expresses in a cry for help. There is a great difference between Christianity and other religious beliefs. For example the Christian has a God who hears and answers prayers. We read about a case with the prophet Elijah and the priest of Baal. A desperate effort was made to speak to their gods by crying out, cutting themselves, but all that did not avail much because the idols had no ability to hear or see (see James 1:6).

How much difference there was when Elijah called on his God, the only true God? He was certain that His God would hear and answer his prayer. The nature of petition is that God has commanded us to pray (Matthew 1:7).

When we pray our petition must be made by faith in the name of Jesus Christ. If these simple rules are followed we can be reassured that our prayer will be heard. According to 1 John 3:22 we should also pray for ourselves, because unless we are in God's will He cannot hear our petition about other things.

We must begin to ask for cleansing says 1 John 1:9, and wisdom. Other areas of our petition will be for the concern of spiritual leaders, says Colossians 4:3, and for sick believers (read what James says to us in chapter 5:14). Directions to pray for rulers and even our enemies are found in Matthew 5:4.

The Lord's Prayer includes making petition for the daily necessities of life. It encourages us to bring our basic needs to Him. There is nothing so insignificant to the Father's care. David states, 'I have been young, and now I am old, yet I have never seen the righteous forsaken or his seed begging bread.' Psalm 37:25

We make petition when we are concerned deeply enough about our own needs and the needs of others, and wish to do something about it. When one comes to God in prayer and petition, we ought to develop a spirit of humility, and desiring nothing, but hoping in God's mercy. We should be ready to respond to the gracious invitation of drawing near, with confidence to the throne of grace, that we may receive mercy and find grace to help in time of need (Hebrew 4:16).

Jesus Made Eight Petitions

The prayer that Jesus prayed in John 17 was not a model prayer like the one He taught His disciples in Matthew 6. This is a prayer of the second person of the Trinity who assumed the human nature. The prayer is addressed to Christ's holy and righteous Father. In this prayer, we will notice, it does not contain any confession of sin. This prayer is unique as that of an obedient Son, who prays for His children.

Jesus had a timetable to carry out while He was on earth. He was always interested in doing the will of His Father no matter what. He showed great love to His disciples and wanted the very best for them, but He knew that there are important issues that must be done before He left to go back to His Father in heaven. Therefore, He made petitions to His Father on behalf of His followers, so that their understanding might be open to the things that He had taught them.

JESUS' FIRST PETITION
In the first petition that Jesus made to His Father, He said 'Father the hour has come, that Glorification is to take place'. The deep passion of His heart was to glorify His Father. Jesus also petitioned the Father to keep His disciples in His name that they might be one as the Father and the Son are one.

SECOND PETITION

When Jesus made the second petition, He prayed, 'O Father glorify me with thine own self with the glory which I had with thee before the world.' Jesus had emptied himself when He became the Goodman (Philippians 2:5). Christ had been tempted in all points as we are tempted: He had known loneliness, hatred, hunger, thirst and sorrow. Now He desired the Father to clothe Him with that power with which He had divested Himself.

THIRD PETITION

In His third petition Jesus made a request to His Father to keep the disciples in His name that they might be one as the Father and the Son are one.

FOURTH PETITION

The fourth request was a petition for unity. There has to be unity among the members of faith, it is absolutely essential. The disciples must be in unity with one another to fulfill what is expected of them when Jesus returns to His father.

FIFTH PETITION

Jesus' fifth petition to the Father had to do with the joy of the church. He prayed, 'That they might have His joy fulfilled in them'. These words were spoken in the presence of the disciples, who were to remain in the world to carry out the work He had called them to do. Their joy was to be completed in Him. Their joy was to be filled to the brim.

SIXTH PETITION

He prayed 'and for their sake I sanctified myself, that they also might be sanctified through the truth'. To sanctify a man is to equip him with the qualities of mind, and heart and character that are necessary for this task. If one is appointed to serve God, He must have some thing of God's goodness and wisdom in him. God called man, and to set them apart, they must seek God's holiness through prayer and the word of God.

SEVENTH PETITION

In the seventh petition, Jesus prayed for perfection of the church in order that the world may know that God had sent Him, that they may be made perfect in one.

EIGHT PETITION

In His eighth petition, Jesus asked His Father that the church be with Him, and share His glory. He was already anticipating the homecoming of the redeemed. Jesus spoke where He would like us to be, namely, in His Father's house. His plan is that we will share with Him the cross and rejoice in God's presence.

David's Petitions And Repentance

Psalms 51

David himself made petitions to God for forgiveness of his sins. David prayed much in the same way as the publican who prayed in the parable of Jesus, 'God be merciful to me a sinner'. He did not rely on former good deeds with his evil doings nor did he think because he was God's servant he would be let off the hook. Rather, he ran to God for His infinite mercy, depending on Him for pardon. David cried 'have mercy on me O God'. David recognized that he had nothing to please God with but depended upon the freeness of His mercy, His loving-kindness, His clemency, the goodness of His nature. God's mercy gives the pardon from sins.

When David sinned he cried, 'Blot out my transgressions'. It was just like having a bad debt crossed out of the book when a debtor has paid the bill in full, or the collector has remitted the debt. David asked God to wash him thoroughly from his iniquity, and to cleanse him from his sin. The prophet Nathan had already reassured David that God had taken away his sin and he would not die (2 Chronicles 12:13).

Nevertheless David prays 'wash me, cleanse me, and blot out my transgressions'. Although God had already forgiven him, David could not forgive himself, so he asked for pardon, washing, cleansing, and the creation of a new heart, and a right spirit.

In David's penitent confession, He was free to own up to his guilt before God. He said, 'I have acknowledged my transgressions.' He had found the way to ease his conscience by confessing his actual regressions. He told God 'against you only have I sinned'. Like David did, it is sometimes best to show the public your repentance, so that others may not think that you are hiding your sins. In addition, David confessed his original corruption when he said 'I was shaped in iniquity' and in sin his mother made him. But sin was not from God's part, we were brought into the world with our corruptive nature, wretchedly, degenerated from its primitive purity and rectitude.

David acknowledged the grace of God and His goodness towards him. He said, 'Thou desire truth in the inward part, in the hidden parts. Thou hast made me to know wisdom'. He believed that truth and goodness go together to make a man good. He was conscious of the uprightness of his heart towards God in his repentance; he had no doubt that God would accept him. He believed that God could make him know wisdom that he could not fall into sin another time.

David prayed that God would purge him and the defilement he had contracted from his sins. He wanted to be cleansed as those who were unclean by the touch of a dead body, by the sprinkling of water, or blood. The expression alluded to a ceremonial distinction that God would reinstate him to his former position as the cleansing of the leper when he is cleansed.

David cried to the Lord and said 'purge me with hyssop'. This is when the blood of Jesus is applied to a sinner's heart by faith, as water of purification was sprinkled with a bunch of hyssop. It is the blood of Christ that is therefore calling the spirit that purges the conscience from dead works, from the guilt of sin, and from God who shuts us out of communion with Him, as the touch of a dead man under the law, that shut a man out from the courts of God's house.

He prayed that his sins would be pardoned. He did not ask for comfort until he was pardoned, that the bitter root of sorrow is taken away, and he prayed in faith. He prayed 'make me to hear joy and gladness'. He cried 'Lord, let me have a grounded peace'. The pain of the heart was broken like broken bones. He needed His spirit of operation to heal and bind up his heart. He prays for a complete and effectual pardon.

As David continued his petitions, he prayed 'Lord, hide thy face from my sin, blot out my iniquity out of thy book of thy account, blot them out as a cloud is blotted out and dispelled by the beams of the sun.' David begged God not to cast him away from His presence. He felt he was good for nothing and could not be looked upon. He cried 'take not thy holy spirit from me'. He knew that he would be undone if the Holy Spirit was taken from him. He knew that if the Holy Spirit had departed from him the consequences he would face would be severe, and therefore begged God earnestly.

He would have preferred to lose his crown, his children, even his life, than not having the Holy Spirit. David prayed to God for restoration, comfort, and the joy of his salvation. A child of God knows that the joy of God's salvation is a good solid joy, so we must take care of what we have; it is our strength in which we live.

When he prayed '*uphold me with thy free spirit*' he meant Lord, I need you to sustain me. My own spirit is not sufficient, if I am left to myself, I will certainly sin. So he cried 'Lord please uphold me'. David promised the Lord that he would teach transgressors the way, because he felt in himself that as he was a transgressor, he would have a lot to teach them from his own experience. David found mercy in the Lord in the way of repentance. He thought that he was in a good position to teach the subject to transgressors. Next David prayed for the sin of blood guiltiness when he killed Uriah with the sword of the children of Amman, with the wrong intention to get his wife.

He promised God that if he delivered him, his tongue would sing aloud of God's righteousness, because God should have the glory for both pardon and mercy. He asked God to open his lips, only to tell sinners about the goodness of God, but his heart would be enlarged in praises. The guilt of sin had closed his lips; therefore he had little confidence towards God. After his relationship was restored he was in a better position to intercede for the people of Zion. This is how true repentance is. It is a good example to follow.

There is only one way that a person can enter into God's kingdom, it is by faith, believing in Christ to save us from sin and change our life. We must do the work of His kingdom to prepare for His return. Jesus also told us how to prepare for life in His eternal kingdom by living a life to please Him now. It is by faith that we will be victorious, overcome all anxieties, and have all negative desires wiped out by the blood of Jesus.

For example, fear, uneasiness, unwanted thoughts that control our minds, lingering thoughts that might want to take up residence in our minds, say with me, *'Be it known to you devil that there is no room for your activities.'* Go to your door and show him where to walk to get out.

We don't have to accommodate his nonsense that constantly plagues our minds.

We should never talk what the devil wants to hear. For instance, some believers will say 'my blood pressure', 'my diabetes', or 'my headache'. Be wise, never claim such illnesses. Although they might be already residing in the body, instead of feeling contented with such conditions, command the sickness to take up its baggage and go in the name of Jesus. We are not in bondage; we are free from the devil's hold. Through the death and the resurrection of our Lord Jesus Christ we are set free. Praise the Lord.

And so, there is therefore no condemnation to those who walk in the spirit. We must make sure that he has not left anything at our address that will urge him to keep coming back to visit. Show him the door once and for all and keep a watch at the door. The angel of the Lord will take up residence at our dwellings, be careful to treat him well.

Once I visited a home and as soon as the door was open there was a large sign written in red behind the entrance door saying, '*Satan the blood of Jesus is against you.*' I thought here is a person who stands against the wicked one; he knows not to even think of entering that house. We must never allow the devil to use us in doing his dirty work for him; neither in thought or actions.

Beware! The devil is a cunning hunter for decent living people. His plan is to pull down, kill and destroy. You may wonder why the devil does not plague his own followers. I believe that because he has already got them in his claws, he feels that they cannot escape from him, but wait until a prayer of deliverance is sent to the throne of grace for the freedom of our loved one. He will have to let them go in the name of Jesus. We must also remind ourselves and others that we have the power to call on the name of Jesus to rescue us from these unhealthy emotions.

The believer has the right through the blood of Jesus to live above, and not beneath. We were transformed by the renewing of our minds. It is only by faith in Jesus that we were transformed to receive a new nature. We must seek to develop a stronger conviction, and trust in the Lord Jesus.

Join me in prayer.

Holy Father, I praise and worship Your great name. Father, I bow in Your presence with great anticipation that You will hear my cry. Father I am petitioning Your divine, grace and mercy for the young men of this nation in the name of Jesus. I ask You in Jesus name to draw them to you, and change the hardness of their heart, and deliver them from the plans of the devil so that they will confess and repent of their sins, and receive You as Lord of their lives. Lord Jesus, please to apply Your blood to conditions that seems impossible to men.

Lord, I also ask You in Jesus name for healing to the troubled, the sick in body, soul, and spirit. Father, I thank You for sending Your word to heal the sick and the suffering, to cast out devils out of those that are possessed. What power and authority there is in the name of Jesus over all conditions. Help us to realize that there is power in the blood of Jesus. Lord God, please apply the blood of Jesus to conditions.

Father You are compassionate, loving, and kind, You cannot fail, and I am taking You at Your word to lift us into Your presence by Your spirit that dwells within us.

I now release my faith in action to the Father, Son and the Holy Spirit for the deliverance of Your people in Jesus name.

Amen.

5

How To Reverence God In Worship

The four and twenty elders fall down before Him who sits on the throne and worship Him who lives forever and ever, and cast down their crowns before the throne, saying, You are worthy, O Lord to receive glory and honor, and power, For You have created all things and by Your will they were created. Revelation 4:10-11.

What is Worship?

Worship generally requires obedience. It also means to bow down, show an act of respect or courtesy in regarding another (Gen 10:31). The purpose of worship is to give us strength and wisdom for service through communication with God. Therefore, giving worship to God should produce positive results, noble character, peace, joy, friendship, righteousness. The church of Jesus Christ was born in an atmosphere of worship, so we must keep our hearts free from the pollution of sin in order to worship the Lord in the beauty of holiness.

The Meaning of Worship: 1 Chronicles 16:29

The word 'worship' refers to the supreme honor given either in thought or deed to a person or thing. The Bible teaches that God alone is worthy of worship. True worship involves at least three elements: *Praise, Adoration and Thanksgiving.* Worship also requires reverence; this includes the honor and respect directly towards the Lord in thought or in feeling. God's word says He seeks that people worship Him in spirit and in truth. John 2: 24 explains the term 'in spirit'. It speaks of the personal nature of worship. It is from my person to God's person and involves the intellect, emotions and will. The phrase 'in truth' speaks of the content of worship. God is pleased when we worship Him, with understanding of His true character.

Worship includes public expression. This was particularly prevalent in the Old Testament because of the sacrificial system. For example, when the believer received a particular blessing for which he wanted to thank God, it was not sufficient just to say it privately, but they wanted to give thanks publicly with an offering (Lev. 7:12). Worship means service. These two concepts are often linked together in scripture. In Deuteronomy 8:19 we read the words for worship in both Testaments, that to do service is linked to the labor of slaves for the master. Worship is especially included in joyful service which Christians render to Christ in their entire life of obedience to God.

Expressions Of Worship

Hebrews 13:15

Worship includes praise and thanksgiving, which may expressed privately or publicly. This can be expressed either by grateful dedication or joyful singing.

Since worship has emphasis in thoughts, feelings, and deeds, there are many other expressions of worship. We express worship by thinking on things that are lovely, pure, and holy. We express our worship through our feelings of compassion for others. We express worship through deeds of kindness, doing the right thing to our fellowmen, knowing that whatever we do it should be done to the glory of God.

A very important memory is for the believers always to be reminded of the death of Christ through the Lord's Supper (1 Corinthians: 11). The Lord's Supper was instituted by Christ himself, see Matthew 26:26.

Since worship means so much to God, it can also be expressed in cheerful giving of money to God's work. This is certainly an act of worship. Also the giving of one's time to the service of the Lord's work maybe considered as worship. See 1 Corinthians 12.

The single and most important act of worship that qualifies the believer is when one presents himself in true obedience to God. The body then becomes the container of the tools by which the will of God is carried out, also the mind because it coordinates the actions to be executed by the body. Romans 1 tell us how to present our bodies as a living sacrifice, holy and acceptable unto God, which is our reasonable sacrifice.

Reasons For Worship

Exodus 2: 3-10

The reason for worship is that God commands us to do so. The first four of the commandments give a clear instruction to men to worship the one and true God, and Him alone. We should not allow any person or thing to usurp the position of lordship over us, this constitutes gross disobedience. An equal and important reason for worship is that God deserves our worship. God alone possesses the attributes that merit our worship and service. Among those are goodness and mercy, holiness, and creative powers (see Exodus 4:31 and Psalms 99:5).

A final reason for worship is because men need to give it to God. People cannot find personal fulfillment apart from submission of themselves in worship in obedience to God, because He is the Creator, and men are the creatures. When people begin to adopt anything as their master instead of God, it is as if they are building their lives on quicksand, it will not last, and it will sink. Men will always seek for someone, or something to worship, because they were created to worship, but true worship must be assigned to God Almighty, He alone is worthy to receive our worship.

Worship then must flow from hearts that are inwardly holy, and outwardly that takes the form of beauty. Worship both deepens and expresses our awareness of God. This element of prayer and deepened awareness results in adoration, thanksgiving, and praise. Spirituality must flow from hearts that are inwardly holy, and outwardly takes the form of beauty. When we worship there is gratitude shown to God and submission to His will. In the worshipping church, there should be a magnificent and triumphant prayer of thanksgiving and intercession. The Psalmist said 'clap your hands all you people, shout for joy unto God with the voice of triumph'.

It will be an amazing outcome if we should learn the secret of power and joy that comes from worshipping in the spirit. During our singing, praying, and body language we are expressing gratitude and appreciation to the Lord. The Psalmist calls us to celebrate God's kingship verbally, full of enthusiasm and intensity; we should give worship with physical imagery and excitement. We should worship joyously; give lively praises to God because He is not a dead God, He is alive forever more.

Worship time is God's time, it is not meant for us to wonder how we look and what people think about us. Never lose focus, for worship belongs to God alone. The Lord takes pleasure in our worship. Sometimes in our corporate worship there maybe times when the worship leader has to pump the audience to worship, but it ought not to be so, everyone should come to church with their individual hearts fired up in praises to God. God will not get any glory from unlovely worship. I always take my Holy Ghost fire stick with me whenever I attend church services. This is because my personal worship starts from home.

Where to Worship God

Our worship can begin in our homes, at church, or other places where born again believers gather in worship and fellowship. Worshipping God together as a family we eventually build up each other. It will remind us that we are all the same Father's children. It helps us to see each other as brothers and sisters in the Lord. There are no high or low grounds; we all have the same responsibility to worship our Father in spirit and truth. We cannot think ourselves more important than others, it is our sovereign Lord who is, it is not 'I, but we'. He is worthy of our worship. 'Thou art worthy O Lord to receive glory and honor and power for thou have created all things, and for thy pleasure they were created'. *Revelation 4:11.*

Worship should flow from a heart of love, where there is little love, there will be little worship. There can also be an element of selfishness even in love. We should, and can worship God in gratitude for what He has done for us, and for who He is, and for the perfection and excellence of His own being. Worship of our Father should embrace every area of our individual life. Paul states that whether we are eating or drinking, or doing anything else we are to do it for God's glory (1 Corinthians 10:31).

Worship then, is the loving ascription of praise to God for what He is, both in himself and in His ways. It is the bowing of the innermost spirit, deep humility and reverence before him. Worship in singing motivates the worshiper before getting into prayer. Singing a devotional song also sets a good mood for worship in church or at home in our private devotions. It would put you into a spiritual atmosphere and encourage worship. Some times as one begins to sing and worship in song, the heart is melted to tears of joy; hands and hearts are lifted to the Most Holy God.

The book of Acts draws back our memory to the times when believers use to get together in the upper room with one accord in prayer and supplication. They were instructed to wait for the promise of the Father. They were to wait ten days for the accomplishment, they gladly obeyed. It is good to be obedient and wait for what is promised. Some times waiting may seem like a long process, and impatience often steps in, but the time can be used to assess oneself, to see if there are any loose ends that need to be tied.

The result of waiting was extraordinary; it yielded a mighty outpouring of the power of the Holy Ghost to enable them for true worship. As empowered men, these worshippers became fire brands that turn the world upside down. They were fearless, they spoke with holy confidence, they were empowered to witness without fear or shame; they had boldness in their worship that was unquestionable.

Prayer, worship and service are what should dominate the Christian life. It is essential if we are to meet the spiritual needs of our fellowmen that it takes the work of the Holy Spirit to create a passion in our personal lives.

God is a spirit and seeks us to worship Him in spirit and in truth. Our worship will be worthless if it is not done in spirit and truth, 'my soul, be thou silent unto God' is the prayer of the Psalmist in Palms 62:5.

A silent word can enshrine a wealth of worship, as when the word '*Rabboni*' fell from Mary's lips *(*John 20: 16).

Worship must be in truth, St John 4:24, that is, one must be free from mere profession of pretence. Therefore to worship God in truth is to acknowledge Him to be who He is, and to know ourselves as men. The idea of worship is common to the whole human race. It means to bow down, or prostrate oneself before God.

Worship is the adoring contemplation of God as He has revealed Himself in Christ and in the scriptures. Worship then is the act of praying in honor and reverence to Almighty God.

Worship is stimulated by remembering that at all times we are in the presence of Almighty God. We ask, how can I know God better so that I can worship Him more worthily? God has granted a partial revelation of Himself in the wonders of nature. The heavens declare the glory of God; the firmament shows His handy work (Psalms 19:1).

All the fullness of the Godhead dwells in bodily-form (Colossians 1:19).

We have often experienced Christ through reading the scriptures, for in them you think you have eternal life. The scriptures are rich in material to feed and stimulate worship and adoration. We are encouraged to read God's word and turn them into prayers. We give God thanks that we have a chance to worship him. Those who are already dead without Christ have missed the opportunity to worship God.

God hates false worship from people who go through the motions out of pretence or for show. If we are living sinful lives and using religious rituals and traditions to make ourselves look good, God will despise our worship, and will not accept the worship that we offer. God wants sincere hearts, and not the songs of hypocrites. When we worship at church, are we more concerned about our image, or our attitude towards God?

Worship in Giving

There are different methods of worship, such as giving our time, money, talents, and abilities, giving ourselves as a living sacrifice, holy and acceptable unto God, which is our reasonable service, as previously mentioned. Giving is a major factor of the Christian life. When worshipping in giving, one should have a cheerful face, a contented mind, and a grateful heart. We are encouraged not to spend our time getting anxious about tomorrow; instead we should give thanks for today even though it might be full of troubles and difficulties.

When we give alms, we should do so discreetly by not letting our left hand know what our right hand is doing. We are told how to give alms, in secret, and our Father who sees in secret himself will reward us openly (Matthew 6:34).

For example, look at our hands how they can be held close together so that if they could see each other, they are aware of what each hand does. So when Jesus said that in giving we should not let one hand know what the other hand is doing, He meant that it should be such a secret that the giver forgets what he gives, and resist making a public show. One should come to terms that giving is before God and not before man.

God sent us His best gift, by giving His only begotten Son Jesus. God gives in abundance; God expects us to give our best in our time, ability, service and giving to others.

If you take the first step in making yourself available to God, He will show us how greatly we can be used to advance the work of His kingdom. When we give to God it does not make Him any richer or poorer, but it makes us more than conquerors. Giving to God and giving to the needs of others is a wonderful activity that we all should be engaged in. It is said that when we give to the poor, we lend to God. Good will comes to the person who lends: God will surely reward us abundantly, press down, shaken together and running over.

One day Jesus was in the temple in the court of women. The treasury was located near, or in the adjoining doorway. There were several boxes put in place which the worshippers could deposit their temple tax and other boxes to collect free will offerings. There was a poor widow who placed a small gift in one of the free will offering boxes. Although it was small, she gave it willingly. The widow gave all that she had to live on, in comparison to the rich who had more but did not choose to give much out of their wealth. What a lesson to think about. It is time to change our motives when we give. We are encouraged to increase our giving, whether in time, money or talent. God, who knows our best, will be pleased when we give our best.

There is no need for one to set a time to give; as the need arises we should do our best to respond in a loving and compassionate attitude (Matthew 10:8).

Some people like to show off in public places to be seen of men when they give. They want everyone to see how good they are at what they can give. We have no need to behave in such a manner when we give. The word of God declares that we should do our alms in secret and our heavenly father will reward us openly. Because giving is a part of worship, we must demonstrate it with joy.

- **Giving should be regular:** persons should always worship God in giving each week; remember to bring an offering when you attend church services.

- **Giving should be cheerful:** our willingness to give cheerfully is more important than the amount that we give. Be happy in spirit when you give to the Lord or give to the needy (Matthew 10:8).

- **Giving must be systematic:** let everyone put aside something tangible, never save back the coppers, but let your heart speak to you on what is acceptable to give.

- **Giving should:** be in proportions as one prospers, it is a key to our growth, in other words the more we give is the more we will receive. God always provides enough to share with others. We should not be mean; ask God for the spirit of giving to come alive within so that you can give willingly.

How does one decide how much to give?

One should give as a response to Christ, and not for what we can get out of it. We should never develop the attitude to swap, it is a good principle to freely receive and freely give; we cannot out-give God. He is the rightful owner of everything. The earth is the Lord's and the fullness thereof, the world and all that dwells therein; He had founded it for himself. If God should decide to take every thing from us can you imagine what would be the outcome? So the next time you feel a grudge coming on remember to share with others what you have received from the Lord and give Him thanks.

It was interesting to read the following short story: A story was told about a Christian woman who had a beautiful flower garden by the roadside. She took great pride to care for her garden. She made sure that the flowers were pruned and watered regularly. It was her custom to give away large quantities of flowers. She would place two large baskets of flowers at her gate. Every morning, she would put fresh flowers in the basket, and those who passed by were invited to help themselves. Tramps, children, and everyone else, who passed by each morning on the way to school, work, and other businesses, took notice and admired the thoughtfulness and kindness of the woman.

The people wondered how on earth it could be, that this woman could be so kind to give away so many flowers which could be sold and make her money.

We remember Brother Judas, who thought that the ointment that Mary poured on Jesus was a waste. Jesus told him to leave her alone and that it was for His burial that Mary anointed Him with the expensive oil. Therefore, this lesson of kindness by this remarkable woman can be put in practice by every one. Let us continue to give, and to do good to others, we never understand the purpose of doing good deeds to others until our Father reveals it.

This kind and thoughtful woman gave so many flowers away without murmuring. When she was asked 'Are you not afraid you will rob yourself by giving away so much?' she replied, 'The more I cut, is the more I have.' Her flower garden has flourished so much. She realized that giving has a place in worshipping God. The more we give away the more room for receiving.

God's giving:

He gives to all men, James 1:5.

God richly provide everything for us to enjoy, 1 Timothy 6:17.

God causes the sun to rise on the evil also on the good, and sends rain on the righteous and on the unrighteous, Matthew 5:43.

He has shown kindness by sending us rain from heaven to water our crops in their seasons. He provides plenty of food and fills our hearts with joy, Acts 14:17.

God gave us a Savior. He sent His Son to be Savior of the world, 1 John 4:14.

God demonstrated His own love for us, in that while we were yet sinners, Christ died for us, Romans 5:8.

The Son of God loved us and gave himself for you and me, Galatians 2:20.

Thanks be to God for His indescribable gift! (2 Corinthians 9:15)

Giving Praise To God

What Is Praise?

Praise is expressing to God our appreciation and understanding of His worth. It is saying, 'O Lord, we respect your divine nature.' Our inward attitude becomes our outward expression when we praise God. We help ourselves by expanding our awareness of who God is. When we read of the praises of David, how he gave praises to God, we should also look for an attribute or characteristic of God in which we too can thank him. Singing praises to God ought to be a continuous part of our lives.

According to 1 Chronicles 16:4 David appointed Levites to minister before the Ark of the Lord, to make petition, to give thanks and to praise the Lord, the God of Israel. We should begin our worship with praise. When the ark of the Lord was brought to the temple; the first service at the temple began with honoring God, and acknowledging His presence and goodness. In the same way our worship should begin by acknowledging God's love. We should praise God first, and then we will be prepared to present our needs to him. Recalling God's love and mercy will inspire us to worship daily.

How Do We Praise God?

All of God's creatures are like a majestic symphony or a great choir that is composed of much harmony that together offer up songs of praise. Each part is independent, yet is a part of the group, caught up and carried along in the swelling tides of praise. This is a picture for believers of how we should praise God, individually, yet a part of the great choir of believers worldwide. We must find our place in this world-choir.

Although the Bible urges us to praise the Lord, most times we are not sure how to go about it. Try praise in dance, with the voice, with musical instruments, see what other ways you can find to praise God.

We are told in Samuel 6:1-15, how David worshipped God in 'bold worship'. It was the only way in which he could give full expression from his heart.

What To Praise God For
There are unlimited benefits to praise God for. He forgets our sins, He heals our diseases, He redeems us from death, He crowns us with love and compassion, satisfies our desires, and gives righteousness and judgment (Psalms 103:1-6).

Listen to the writers of the Book of Romans and also Psalms in the expression of praises to God. Romans 11:37 states, 'O the depth of the riches and wisdom and knowledge of God, how unfathomable are His judgment, how undiscovered are His ways.'

The Lord is Glorious. O, the glorious splendor of His MAJESTY. David said 'I will mediate on all His wonders works'.

The Lord is Gracious. He is gracious and full of compassion. He is slow to anger and abounding in mercy and loving-kindness. The Lord is Good- He is good to all, and His tender mercies are all over world, in the entire work of His creation.

The Lord is Righteous. He is righteous in all His ways. He is gracious, and merciful in all His ways. The Lord is worthy to be praised, from the rising of the sun, the Lord's name is to be praised (Psalms 113:3).

'The Lord is Holy. He is near to all who calls on him, to all who call upon him, in sincerity and truth,' declares Psalm 145:18. 'For great is the Lord, His greatness is pondered by all who delight in him. He causes His wonders to be remembered, glorious and majestic are His deeds.'

A lot more can be found in the Psalms of David, a man who knew how to really praise the Lord. He emphasized, 'Let everything that has breath praise the Lord.'

Praise will open locked doors and set captives free, praise will lighten your burdens.

Praise will confuse the enemy and cause him to run in terror, praise will drive out the enemy out of your space. Praise will allow you to look beyond your limitation, and see Jesus standing at the Father's right hand saying, 'Hold on my child, joy comes in the morning'.

What The Lord Does:
He upholds. The Lord raises those who are fallen and bowed down.

He gives. The eyes of all wait on him, He gives them their meat in due season.

He **satisfies.** The Lord opens His hands and satisfies every living thing with His favor.

The Lord **makes** springs pour water into deserts, to give water to feed the thirsty.

He fulfills. The Lord will fulfill and preserve all those who love him.

Psalms says, 'I will **extol** the Lord with all my heart in the council of the upright.'

Join me in prayer.

Our God, our Father, I come to You in the name of our Lord Jesus Christ, O, how I worship Your great and wonderful name. Your name is powerful, Your name is mighty, and Your name will drive away all fears. You are the God of Abraham, Isaac, and Jacob, they trusted in You and they were not ashamed. You brought them out of many afflictions, Father we give You praise.

Father God, I give You praise, because of Your goodness that is past finding out. Lord, right now I bow in Your presence in faith believing that You are with me, according to Your promise that You will never leave or forsake me.

Father, I stand on Your promises to fulfill what You have said. I bring sacrifice of praise from a heart of thanksgiving; please accept the praise offering that I offer in Jesus name. Father, in Jesus name I bring to You all my dreams and aspirations. Father, I ask for Your help so that I will keep focused on the things that are needful and necessary.

Please remember those who are reading the pages of this book, O Lord. Shine the light of Your countenance on each chapter so that the truth of Your words may come alive on every page. Lord, it is all about You and Your will for our lives. Shine Jesus... shine through.

Lord, I adore You in all Your heavenly splendor and I pray that You will keep that which I have committed to You in Your safekeeping. I ask these mercies in Jesus name.

Amen

6

Intercession

If anyone among you is sick let him call for the elders of
the church and let him pray over him, anointing him with oil
in the name of the Lord (James 5:14).

There is nothing in the Christian faith quite as effective as intercession. It is the way that leads to the winning of souls. No church can prosper without it, and no Christian can grow without it. The law of life demands reproduction, that kind should beget kind. In the same way that a church needs to develop a Prayer Program, it is the same way that a church should have an Evangelism Program up and running effectively.

According to Isaiah 53: 12, Jesus intercedes for all. He has left the charge with us to carry on (Matthew 9:38).

James 5:13 encourages us to pray in all situations. He said, 'If any one is afflicted let him pray, any sick, let him call for the elders of the church to pray over him, anointing him with oil in the name of the Lord.' He said that the prayer of faith shall save the sick, and the Lord shall raise him up, and if he has committed any sins they shall be forgiven. This includes, for example, physical ailments, personal traits, spiritual battles, or any other troubles, the advice is to pray in faith. When we are in trouble we have a tendency to believe that our problems will not be solved, but be encouraged, troubles will not last, and our God understands our situation.

Many saints have experienced the power of intercessory prayer. They demonstrate the method of prayer like a mighty weapon to conquer the enemy and bring glory to God. The life of a witness is counted as barren and ineffective without the power of intercessory prayer. The power of intercessory prayer is more beneficial to believers than a church with a hundred members but no knowledge of how to intercede for others. Prayer crowns God with honor and glory that is due to His name, while God crowns the believer who prays with assurance and comfort. A church without holiness would be like a social club, where people gather for entertainment and leave with a sense of emptiness.

Intercession is when we are concerned with the needs and interests of others. It is the unselfish attitude of prayer. It means to fall in with a person, to draw near, so that we can converse freely and have access. It is a word used to describe a child going to his father on behalf of another or a person who enters the king's presence to submit a petition.

In intercession the believer is acting as an intermediary between God and man. He forgets himself and his needs and identifies with the needs of the other who he prays for.

To make intercession to God on behalf of others is both a privilege and the responsibility of every Christian. It is so important that Christians pray in faith for themselves and for the unsaved, families, friends and enemies, that God's marvelous light would shine in their hearts and bring them to repentance. It is vitally important to witness to people about life after death. This is an urgent need that should never be put off. People need to decide in this life where they want to be in the life after death. Therefore, it is imperative that the believer takes the message of salvation and shares it with those who they come in contact with.

Another important service is to pray for them, and with them, we are to urge them of the dangers of neglecting the Savior. We must be aware that this life is just a period of preparing for the life to come. How we live here on earth will determine where we will be in the hereafter. In this life it is a daily preparation, each day we have to seek to keep our hearts in perfect peace and our minds stayed on God. It is always needful and good to keep an evaluation on our own selves to find out how we are doing. Just in case we preach to others and at the end we hear, 'depart from me, I know you not'.

At that final day there will be no time for making excuses or for debate; what is done will not be undone. Therefore while we have the opportunity let us use it wisely and remind others, and also ourselves to do likewise… living harmoniously as children of one Father, which is our Lord and Savior Jesus Christ, who is coming back again to give every man according as his works shall be. We ask God for His forgiveness, and confess all known sin, and repent, never to do them again; then we should give Him thanks, worship and adore Him for His unmerited favor. Sometimes I think we should just give praises to God and omit begging for things only to satisfy our wants. There is a time for everything, so be wise and put God first in our prayers and He will grant our most urgent request.

Christ's return sometimes seems like a forgotten dream, because there is not much emphasis that is put on the second coming of the Lord. There are all kinds of recreation, social gathering and entertainment, and there is not much being said about the Lord's return. We must be mindful about this important issue, and turn up the volume, hoping that some evangelist would come and remind and stir the hearts of both believers and sinners of the return of our Lord. When you are fully engaged in prayer, the spirit of the Lord will be aroused, and enlighten our desire to come alive in the reality that Christ is coming back to earth again. Every eye shall see Him as He is.

Reader, would you be pleased to meet the Savior when He comes? Or have you forgotten that He is coming back? Let us think and talk about it more often, let us keep it on our priority list. Talking about lists, we must keep the lamp of intercession burning at all times, for we know not the day or the hour when our Lord will come.

The word of God says that He will come as a thief in the night. When we feel that all is well it will be like sudden destruction. Let us remind each other to be ready and waiting for the King of Glory. The triumph of God shall sound and the dead in Christ shall rise first and those who are alive shall be caught up together with Him in the air. And so shall we be with Him. That is what I call a time of excitement, but it will also be a time of weeping for those who have rejected the gospel, and those who are not ready to meet and to greet the savior. We are told to comfort one another with these words. Until then, we will continue to find the effectiveness in prayer.

David's prayer, according to Psalms 119: 6-9, was an intercessory prayer on behalf of others. Too often we are quick to pray for own needs and desires, and omit interceding for others. The peace that is sought in theses verses is more than an absence of conflict, and protection. The world is unable to provide this peace, but the real peace comes from faith in God, because He alone embodies all the characteristics of peace.

Therefore, the first and most important concern and act of prayer should be for the spiritual well-being of every individual. Our main concern should be for the saving of souls to secure an eternal future. In so much that in some cases the sinner is unable to recognize that he is lost and is in need of a savior. All prayer should be offered in faith for he who comes to God must believe that He hears and is the answerer of our prayers according to His will.

When one makes intercession there are reflex benefits to the one who prays as well as the one on whose behalf intercession is made. In times of inward dryness and desperation God is always too pleased to hear our heart's cry on behalf of others in intercessory prayer. Oh! Wouldn't it be soul inspiring if we were to hold out the torch of prayer high in intercession on behalf of others!

Some Effective Prayers That Have Touched Lives

ABRAHAM'S prayer in Genesis 18:23-33

When Abraham interceded to God for the people of Sodom, he asked God, 'Wilt thou destroy the righteous with the wicked?' God heard his prayer and delivered Lot and his family from the destruction of Sodom.

MOSES' prayer in Exodus 32:11

Moses sought the Lord and said, 'Lord, why doest thy wrath wax hot against thy people, which thou hast brought forth out of the land of Egypt, with great power and with a mighty hand?' He said, 'Lord, remember Abraham, Isaac, and Israel, your servants to whom you swore by your own self and said to them, saying 'I will multiply your descendants like the stars of heaven, and all this land that I have spoken of I will give to your descendants, and they shall inherit it forever'.' God heard that prayer and answered.

JACOB'S prayer in Genesis 31

How would you feel knowing you were about to meet the person you had cheated out of his most precious possession? Jacob had taken Esau's birthright and his blessing. Now he was about to meet this brother for the first time in 20 years and he was frantic with fear. However Jacob turned his worries into prayers. He collected his thoughts and decided to pray. When we face difficult conflicts we can run about frantically or we can stop to pray. Which approach will be more effective?

So Jacob wrestled with an angel at Bethel, and he said to God, 'Deliver me, I pray, from the hand of my brother, Esau, for I fear him, lest he come and smite me, and the mothers with the children.'

It was during the night that Jacob received a message from the Lord that told several things. He continued to rehearse how the Lord had been very good to his father Abraham and Isaac. He repeated that the land which God had promised to his father would be his one day, that his seed would be innumerable like the dust of the ground spreading to the four corners of the earth: and through his descendants, all the people of the earth would be blessed. For this, he was assured, God would keep him wherever he went, and although he was now leaving the land of promise, God would someday bring him back to it.

God would never leave him until he had fulfilled in his life all of His promises. When Jacob awoke from his sleep he said, 'Surely the Lord is in this place and he knew it not.'

(Genesis 28:16) This stated how carnal Jacob had been in his past life, but he recognized that he was now in the divine presence of Almighty God. So if God can fix Jacob's past life of deception and other trickery attitude, surely He will fix anyone's past if we ask Him (see Genesis 32:9).

JABEZ'S prayer in Judges:

JABEZ **is** remembered for his prayer request rather than a heroic act. In his prayer he asked God to bless him, to help him in his work, to enlarge his territory, to be with him in all he did, and to keep him from evil and harm. Jabez acknowledged God as the true centre of his work. When we pray for God's blessing, we should also pray that He will take His rightful position as Lord over our family, time, and recreation. We need to understand that obeying God is our individual responsibility that is not transferable. It is our own duty. So many times we repeat the prayer of Jabez; it is unique, and should be applied to our lives.

JOSHUA'S prayer in Joshua 8

When Joshua claimed the victory at Jericho, he tore his clothes, and fell on the earth upon his face before the ark of the Lord, and until evening, he and the elders of Israel put dust on their heads (Joshua 7: 6).

Joshua commanded the people saying, 'You shall not shout, nor make any noise with your voice, neither shall any word proceed out of your mouth, until the day when I bid you shout.' The people were to march around the city of Jericho in silence. The silence spoke volumes; it testified to onlookers of faith in God, there is nothing as impressive as silence.

The people obeyed Joshua as their leader with anticipation and waited for another miracle like the one when they crossed the Red Sea. Although they marched in silence, their faith was in action. Perhaps as they marched, they were silently praying to God to keep them faithful and true. As they repeated the marching operation the people were pressed to trust God, they had Him on their minds and that made the marching much easier. At last when they were commanded to shout, the wall came tumbling down. We can take lessons from this silent march of faith and watch our walls of difficulty, depression, despair or any other wall, come down in the mighty name of Jesus Christ.

ELIJAH'S prayer in 1 Kings 9

When the prophet Elijah prayed for a widow's son, he cried to the Lord and said, 'O Lord my God, have you brought tragedy on this widow that I am staying with by causing her son to die?' Then He stretched himself on the boy three times, and cried to the Lord God to allow the boy's life to return to him. God heard Elijah's cry, the boy's life was returned to him, and he lived (1Kings 17:20).

Elijah's prayer at Mount Carmel was so overwhelming and shows that the true God literally answers by fire.

JESUS' prayer in John 17

Jesus' prayers have also played an integral part in His earthly ministry. He is our prime example, because although Jesus had the authority and power over all things He still devoted a lot of His time in prayer to His heavenly Father. If Jesus saw the need to pray, how much more should we humans have reasons to pray? We commit sins everyday in our thoughts, words, actions, with our eyes and various other areas that cannot be counted.

Therefore prayer is a necessary tool to put us back in line with our heavenly Father. Our fellowship with the Father needs to be in communion and fellowship with the believers also in order for a healthy Christian lifestyle to be accomplished. We must make it possible to pray without delay... we must seek to grow and develop a strong prayer life that will sustain us through the storms of life.

The Importance Of Praying For Others

James 4:16

It is of great importance to pray and show brotherly love to one another, especially to believers in the Lord. We must make it our duty to pray for the church, the leaders, members, families, political leaders in government and other countries; as a matter of fact, we have a great responsibility to pray and not to faint. Pray about the awful conditions that they face, especially when making decisions in leadership. Church leaders in particular are men and women who watch over our souls.

They need our prayers to carry out the will of God effectively. We should pray for ministers of the gospel regularly, pray with them, and for them. We will be considered as doing the will of God. We may not be able to travel where they go to minister but our prayers will mean a lot to them. Church leaders need to continue growing in their spiritual life and have the ability to lead, and also to equip others to grow and develop.

Some people will accept our prayers graciously and openly and even admit that they have needs to be met, but may not be willing to take the time to pray for themselves. There are those who readily reject the invitation of Christ, or may even resent to be prayed for; in some cases these include those who are in desperate need of help, to change.

The devil will put up roadblocks to hinder people to come out of their stronghold and accept the truth and give their lives to Jesus. So the one that is praying must be aware that sometimes a person genuinely wants to give up but they are tied up so tightly that it will only take a discerning spirit with the blood of Jesus to loose such one and commit them to the Lord.

We must believe that it is the Spirit that draws people to the Lord. But the need of a Savior remains the same, man needs God and to get back in fellowship with Him.

For example, when we are young we think that life is forever. We never think that we will get old and die. However, sooner or later we come learn that it is appointed unto man once to die and after death comes the judgment. For all our deeds we will be called to give an account. Whether they are good or bad, we will be judged accordingly. Since this is the case, the wisest thing that we can do and advise others to do, is to repent, and ask God to forgive us of all our sins and have fellowship with God, before it is too late. It takes preparation to meet Jesus Christ, the one who died for us.

This is the reason I decided to write about this subject of prayer. It is a necessary subject to employ in our daily activities, accompanied with reading and studying the word of God. It will help us to see ourselves more clearly, how much we need God's cleansing everyday of our lives, and remind us to prepare to meet Jesus Christ, the one who died for us, because we cannot enter heaven with any sort of sin.

Young people often think they have a lot of time and put off this most important duty for a later date, after they have achieved their education, personal goals and all the achievements that life calls for. There is absolutely nothing wrong with being ambitious, but remember it is only what is done for Christ that will last. One day we will look in the mirror and see wrinkled skin and grey hairs... but, ah, time waits for no one.

The word of God says that if we hear His call today we should not harden our hearts. We should remind the youth that now is the time to serve the Lord, for if they should visit the cemetery there are people of all ages.

Concerning older persons they are sometimes more readily to accept the gospel rather than putting it off. Summing up their past they recognize that time is not in their favor. As people grow older, they tend to be more conscious of what will happen to them after leaving this world. They may take it seriously or treat it as a passing thought that will soon wear off. Surely that is a major concern; indeed everyone should take this approach seriously, and ask, 'Where do I go from here?' They may even try to seek a way that leads to happiness and peace, but there is only one way to life eternal.

Everyone has the unique quality and inherent nature that recognizes there is a God, a supreme being who should be served. People always have various needs and are desperate for someone to pray for them. Some will not even take the time to pray for themselves, but are anxious for someone to take the responsibility to pray for them. It is okay to pray for others, but we should encourage them to start a life of prayer for themselves. We should understand that prayer is the connection line that leads to the throne of grace.

There is a line that runs from here to there; it must be free from all blockages on our part. This line can be blocked by all sorts of debris: known sin, hidden sins, resentments, pride and more. We must make it our duty to keep the line free. We have to be mindful and to daily check to ensure that the line is clear in case of an emergency when we need to get help from above. So in the natural, so it works in the spiritual. There can be line-cross from the enemy of our souls.

We have been given the authority by our Lord Jesus Christ to rebuke Satan, and cast him out of our affairs and conversation with our Father. He acts as an unwanted intruder. I do not wish to exalt him in this book; nevertheless we should not be ignorant of his devices. He always tries to interfere in our fellowship, especially when it is time to pray, we must be determined to rebuke, resist and push him out and plead the blood of Jesus against him. He will cast disruption on our health, by allowing our minds to be taken up with his negatives thoughts, action towards others – so be aware.

One cannot pray effectively for others until personal acceptance has been gained through confession of known sins. When we get it right with the Father then we can launch out in prayer for ourselves and others.

For example when Isaiah went to visit Hezekiah, who was extremely ill, and told him of his impending death, Hezekiah immediately turned to God in prayer. God responded to his fervent prayer. Hezekiah lived another fifteen years in respond to fervent prayer. God may change the course of our lives too; we should never hesitate to ask God for radical changes. We must remember to honor him when we receive divine favor from him.

According to 2 Chronicles, Hezekiah had a problem with pride even after his double miracle of healing and deliverance. Eventually he and his subjects humbled themselves, so God's judgment was put off for several more generations. When Hezekiah realized that his prayer brought deliverance and forgiveness, he confessed that the grave cannot praise God, he knew that God had spared his life for His purpose.

It is a comforting thought to hear someone say 'I am praying for you'. It gives a spiritual enlistment to the spirit and encouragement to the heart. In the Word of God this is one of the commands, that Christians should pray for one another, for people everywhere, for rulers, governors, people in distress, for young and old, remembering someone once prayed for us. Paul says, 'I ceased not to give thanks for you, making mention of you in my prayers'. His desire and prayer was that God would continue to work in them, in the revelation to express the need to learn special lessons and insight that only God can supply.

In acknowledgement of the goodness of God, we are privilege to gather information and teachings about the things of God, some of these are rooted in Paul's prayers; he often spoke of the unmerited favor of God. It is the grace that appears to all men, teaching them to avoid ungodly living and turn their lives to God.

We can also enjoy this wonderful experience in prayer. As we take the time to devote ourselves and seek the Lord in prayer, our meditation will be sweet. We will enjoy His presence with unspeakable joy. As we humbly pray, 'Let us hear the conclusion of the whole matter: fear God and keep His commandments for this is the whole duty of man. God will bring every work into judgment with every secret thing, whether it is good or evil.' (Ecclesiastes 12:13-14)

Try including these elements in your prayer:

Praise... Lord we praise Your Holy name, Oh Lord, we bless Your great name.

Worship... Lord we bow down before You in obedience and worship.

Adoration... Lord I adore You as Lord of my life, how excellent is Your name.

Confession... Father I confess my sins and ask for pardon.

Petition... Lord Jesus Christ, I make petition for my son, daughter, my unsaved friends, and my enemies, to be saved in Jesus Christ's name.

Supplication... Lord Jesus Christ, I am making this supplication on the behalf Your ministering servants, please hedge them in.

Thanksgiving... Lord we thank You for all that You have done.

Forgiveness... Father we accept Your forgiveness and pardon for our sins.

Join me in prayer.

Father, I come into Your presence this day in the name of Jesus Christ. This is the day that You have made; I thank You for Your daily bread that You have provided. Holy Father, I just want to love You for coming into my life at a time when I thought all hope was gone, thank You for rescuing me out of the jaws of the adversary. Father, I give You praise, Hallelujah.

Jesus I thank You for Your kindness and Your goodness and I do appreciate everything that was done on my part and for others. Here Lord, take my heart, it is an empty vessel, fill it with thy grace and love.

Father God, I thank You for giving me peace with myself and with others. What a wonderful plan of salvation that You have wrought within me through the blood of Jesus' death on the cross. Lord, I lift my hands towards Your holy heavens in adoration and thanksgiving.

Father, I ask that Your abiding peace be ever mine, I ask that the same peace that passed all understanding may be active in the lives of my brothers and sisters in the Lord.

Father, I believe Your word that states that if I ask anything in Your name You will do it according to 1 John 14 verse 14. And so I ask these mercies in the name of Your beloved Son Jesus.

Amen

7

Thanksgiving

Philippians 4:6

The next element in prayer is thanksgiving, which is the glad appreciative acknowledgement of the benefits and blessings that God gives. Thanksgiving always flows from a heart of gratitude that can permeate towards us or to others. The important and spiritual benefit of thanksgiving in our prayers cannot be over emphasized. The Bible also says that God resists the proud, but He gives grace to the humble. We can be humble by being thankful, or cheerful, and not being worried for anything, but prayerful in all things.

Thanksgiving should be distinguished from worship. It is not so much occupied with the perfection of God, as it is the acknowledgement of the love and kindness that He has lavished on us. Thankfulness is a magical element that both produces and has an element of happiness. There are so many things for which to be thankful: life, salvation, protection, air, water, food, clothes shelter, friends, and the ability to see, to smell, to hear, and to feel, overall that is for ME.

We are called upon to develop this common courtesy to be thankful, seeing that we are constantly at the receiving end of God's generosity. Even in our own personal lives we take it as a good practice to say thanks to our fellowmen when we receive something from them. We should be so much more thankful to our heavenly Father who will fill us up with His blessings.

It is a sin to be unthankful. This is the sin that cause the Ancient world to plunge into the terrible depth of sexual depravity. In the Old Testament priests were set apart for nothing else but to praise and give thanks to God, see 2 Chronicle 31:2.

Thanksgiving should not be difficult especially when it flows from recognizing temporal and spiritual blessings that we consider desirable. However, when we have experienced suffering and the burdens of life it would seem that giving thanks is the last thing we ought to do. We willingly give thanks when all is going smooth, but God is expecting His children to give thanks for everything at all times (see Ephesians 5:20 and 1 Thessalonians 5:18).

We do not suggest that it is easy, but with the help of the Lord it is possible. It was said by an Arab proverb that 'All sunshine makes a desert'. Our Father knows the exact proportion with which to mix these ingredients for His children.

Thanksgivers:

The Psalmist encourages us to give thanks unto the Lord, 'for He is good and His mercies endure for ever'. He also reminds us that as we bless the Lord from our souls we should 'forget not all His benefits' (Psalms 102:2).

Here the writer's heart overflows with thanksgiving and praises as he meditates on the theme of God's goodness. David gave thanks and did not forget God's benefits.

The prayers of our Lord Jesus Christ was not lacking in giving thanks to His Father on many occasions. Jesus gave thanks to the Father even at the grave of Lazarus. He looked up and said, 'Father, I thank you that you have heard me. I know that you always hear me, but I said this for the benefit of the people standing here, that they may know that you have sent me.' (John 11:41)

Even before He fed the five-thousand-strong-crowd, Jesus gave thanks for the loaves He distributed to the disciples, who in turn distributed them to those sitting down. He did likewise with the fish, and the people were able to eat as much as they wanted (John 6: 11).

When the 70 disciples returned with gladness, Jesus told them that they should not rejoice because devils were subject to them, but to rejoice because their names were written in the Book of Life. Jesus rejoiced in the spirit and said, 'I praise you Father, Lord of heaven and earth, that you have hidden these things from the wise and prudent and revealed them to babes. Even so Father for it seemed good in your sight.' (Luke 10:21)

When Jesus instituted the Lord's Supper, He took the bread, gave thanks, broke it, and gave it to the disciples saying, 'This is my body which is given for you, and do this in remembrance of me.' (Luke 22:19)

We are reminded how the Lord deals with us, His children; His mercies are new every morning and great is His faithfulness. (Lamentation 3:22-23)

I read a story of a missionary who was greatly discouraged in his ministry. He knew that his work was not progressing as it should, even though he put so much time and effort in striving for improvement. One day while visiting another missionary, he saw a motto that was placed on a wall saying, TRY THANKSGIVING!

Thanksgiving!

This message was like an arrow to his soul. It pierced deep within his heart. He went home and began to think about what it meant. It was suddenly revealed to him that an element had been missing from his prayer life. There had been plenty of asking God for things he desired and needed. He had asked desperately at times, but had forgotten to give thanks for what he received. His attitude was changed. He began to count his blessings and pour out his heart in thanksgiving to God.

From then on the power of the Spirit began to search through him, and show him where he was lacking.

After applying this element of thanksgiving in his prayer, he noticed that the work of his missionary centre began to prosper. People began to get saved. He then could share his experience with the other believers concerning what had happened to his ministry. It is so good for brethren to dwell together in unity, but some had already left the ministry because of the dryness that existed in the congregation. In times of failures we must remain faithful in good relationship with the leader that everything will work together for good to them that love the Lord. We must be prepared to stay the course until the light shines again.

Some believers accepted the challenge and also develop a grateful heart giving God thanks, in worship. The leader's lack of thanksgiving had been quenching the work of the Holy Spirit. He had left out this precious element in his prayer and suffered the sequences of not having a growing church. Thanksgiving is one of the vital ingredients that make up the whole. It is like baking a cake and putting all the ingredients in, then mixing them all together to give a finger-licking taste. We cannot afford to be lacking in worship, praise, and thanksgiving; only then are we provided with all the elements we need. Let us apply them with joy, then we will draw water out of the well of salvation.

When our inner longing for righteousness is satisfied, it will be reflected in our outward character and conduct. God is pleased for those who have a healthy and hearty appetite for the things pertaining to his glory. Let us ask God to make us hungry for him, less of us and more of Him, until we are completely lost in His love. Praise is belonging to God.

A thankful heart has no room for bitterness, hostility, hatred, or spite. You can trust God that all things will work together for good to them that love him, to them that are called according to His purpose (Romans 8: 28). In every situation of life, give thanks for this is the will of God in Christ Jesus concerning you (1 Thessalonians 5:8).

Have we been guilty of the same sin of un-thankfulness?

Think of how God is consistently providing for His people, but people refuse to see what He has done. They show no interest in thanking him. The sin of ungratefulness is commonly among men.

When did you last thank your parents for caring for you? Your pastor for the service he gives to your church? Your child's teacher for the care given each day in activities? Your heavenly Father for His guidance? Many of the benefits and privileges we enjoy are the result of loving actions that were done a long time ago. Someone prayed for you, maybe a loving mother's prayer, or someone else who really cared. Let us look for acts of love and thank those who make it happen.

Let us restart our godly efforts to practice thankfulness, as we ask the Holy Spirit to guide and teach us how to be thankful. Say 'thank you' and really mean it. It gives encouragement to the other party. Prayer, praise and thanksgiving walk hand in hand, they are loving sisters. They who have praises will have virtues in prayer.

John Newton, the converted slave trader, used to give thanks as a practical 'twist' by saying 'that true thanksgiving is thanks living'.

Join me in prayer.

Father, I come to You in the name of Jesus, to thank You for health and strength and the daily blessings that You have provided. Father, You are so good and Your mercies endure forever. O Lord, my soul rejoices in the God of my salvation.

Father, I bring the family to Your throne of grace. I ask You heavenly Father to help us to love each other as You have loved us and gave yourself to ransom us from sin.

Lord, I give You praise. Please forgive us of the sins of neglect, let it never have dominion over us but let us ever be mindful of each other, especially those of the household who are facing problems in the family.

Father God, we realize that we cannot do any thing to earn Your pardon and peace but it's only through Your grace and Your mercies. You have said in Your word that if we confess and forsake our sins, You are willing to forgive and to cleanse us from all unrighteousness.

Thank You Holy Father, for the transformation You have provided for our redemption. I ask these mercies in Jesus Christ's name.

Amen

8

Personal Requirements

Purity In Heart:

The pure in heart shall see God. This is the most comprehensive character of the Beatitudes. The true Christian will live in the purity of the heart. The heart must be pure in opposition to mixture. It must be free from pollution, or defilement, as wine unmixed, and as water in undiluted. The heart must be kept from all filthiness of the flesh and spirit. The heart must be purged by faith and entirely clean for God. No wonder the Psalmist cried 'create in me a clean heart, O God, and renew a right spirit within me' (Psalms 51:10).

The Psalmist states, 'If I regard iniquity in my heart the Lord will not hear.' Our confession of sins must be continual because we continue to do wrong. He confessed his sin and prayed, 'forgive my hidden faults, keep your servant from willful sins' (Psalm 19:12 and Psalms 66:1519).

We must cultivate purity of heart. The heart is likened to a field, if the farmer wants to get good crops, he has to maintain and keep the soil free from obstruction, weeds, and all the things that would cumber growth in the field. He has to take the time to keep it moist by regularly tending and watering it.

Jesus said blessed are the pure in heart for they shall see God. Keeping your hands from sin and a pure heart is generally a good attitude to start with. We must show a heart of forgiveness towards others; this is our first requirement in prayer. For if you forgive men when they sin against you, your heavenly Father will also forgive you. If you do not forgive men their sins, our Father will not forgive our sins (Matthew 6:14, 15).

When we take the time to bury the hatchet and make up with those who have done us wrong, or with whom we have done wrong, we will find out that life will begin to progress. The light of God's presence will shine through more brightly. We ourselves will be benefited greatly. The weight of sin will be lifted, and we will be able to raise our hands to the Father without looking over our shoulders or feeling guilty.

There are times when we should leave our gifts at the altar, then go and make it right with those with whom we had a quarrel, then come and present our gifts at the altar. God will answer our prayers when we genuinely forgive. Certain important conditions must be met in order for our prayers to be effective and move mountains. We must be true believers, and we must not hold a grudge against another person.

The Bible urges us to 'put on tender mercies, kindness, humility, meekness, longsuffering, even as Christ forgave us, so we must do' (Colossians 3:12-13).

We should not pray with selfish motives. Our requests should always be for the good of God's kingdom. To pray effectively we need to have faith, not so much in the object of our request, but in what God can do for us.

Believing In Christ's Name

John 13:14

We must believe in our heart that Jesus Christ is the Son of God, that He suffered and died on the cross of Calvary, and that He was buried but He rose again, and is now seated at the right hand of His Father in heaven.

We must confess it with our mouth, tell some body, and let them hear from us the truth about what we believe. We must believe in Christ's name, His name is above every other name. There is no other name under the sun whereby a sinner can be saved from his sins. It is such a powerful name, that at the name of Jesus Christ every knee will bow and every tongue will confess that Jesus Christ is Lord. The people in Jesus' time on earth did not believe Him despite the miraculous signs He performed, and as a result God hardened their hearts. He simply confirmed their own choices as a result of resisting God. They became so set in their ways that they would not even try to understand Jesus' message. For such people, it is ritually impossible to come to God, because their hearts have been permanently hardened, see Exodus 9:12 and Romans 11:7.

What a Name!

It's a lovely name. It has with it a calming remedy that soothes our troubled hearts, it heals our brokenness, it comforts and cheers, it gives assurance to the doubtful that all is not lost; there is still hope for a second chance.

At the name of Jesus Christ all hell runs in terror, and demons tremble. As believers in Christ who confess the name of Jesus, He has given to us the authority to use His name. It is a grand privilege that is afforded to us; as long as we live up to the responsibility of the name it will be effective when we use it. There are so many benefits in the name of Jesus. It brings cleansing, salvation, healing, deliverance, freedom, freshness, it soothes our aching hearts, it brings relief from worry and unrest, comfort to troubled minds, it shines light in darkness, and much more.

Everyone has a right to believe in something, or someone, but is that thing or person able to deliver in time of trouble? It is not enough only to believe, but we must be fully persuaded that He is able to keep that which we have committed to Him. We must also believe that we can put all our trust in Him at all times.

According To Christ's Will:

1 John 5:14

The matter of our prayers must be agreeable to the declared will of God. Jesus himself was obedient to pray according to the will of His father. At a crucial moment in His suffering in agony, He prayed that not His will but the will of the Father may be done.

According to 1 John 5:14, 'this is the confidence that we have in Him, that if we ask any thing according to His will, He will hears us'. We must pray according to the will of God. Sometimes we are prone to pray with our own will already in place, then when disappointment comes we ask God to take over, but it should not to be so.

True faith in God will generate kindness, compassion, justice, and humility. We can please God by requesting His help in our family, our work, our church, and with our neighbor. We cannot ask God for help when we ignore those who are needy and oppressed, while we silently condone the action of those who oppress them. Micah 6:8 states, 'We showed you, O man, what is good, and what the Lord requires of you, is to act justly, and to love mercy, and to walk humble with your God.'

To save time, effort and disappointment, it is a good idea to ask God in the first place, what His will is. The word of God says 'that we should seek first the kingdom of heaven and all other things will be added to us'. One way of knowing God's will for our lives is to constantly read and meditate on His word, and walk in obedience. Prayer is another element to find God's will. Let us seek to know the will of God in submission to him so that His will be done in our lives. When we know and understand His will, we will be able to pray effectively. It is wise to go to God and ask Him what His will is.

God is the best person to ask. When we are faced with burning desire, He will answer our request. Think about it carefully. If Jesus, who is the Son of God, chose to satisfy the will of His father when He could have chosen to use His own will, then we must learn what this is saying to us as believers. We ought to find out the will of God and in obedience do what His word says to us (1 John 5:14). While Jesus was praying He was aware of what doing the will of His Father would cost him. He understood the suffering that He was about to encounter, but He prayed, 'not my will, but what your will'. Anything that is worth having will cost something.

When Jesus prayed in the Garden of Gethsemane, He fell to the ground and prayed that if it be possible that the hour might pass from him. 'Abba Father,' He said, 'everything is possible for you to take this cup from me, yet not what I will, but what you will'. One can think within themselves this question: Was Jesus trying to get out of His task? No, He was expressing His true feelings, but He did not deny or rebel against His Father. He reaffirmed to do what God wanted. Jesus' prayer heightens the terrible suffering He had to endure, an agony so much magnified, because He had to take on the sins of the world (Mark 11:35).

Join me in prayer.

O God, You are our help in ages past, our years to come, and our shelter from the stormy blast, and our eternal home. Father, we thank You for Your sheltering arm that has carried us through the rough times, and the good times, how much we give You praise.

Lord, help us to always remember where You have taken us from and where we could have been.

Thank You for cleansing in the blood of Jesus Christ. Father, all the deep-rooted sins that seem to linger in our thoughts, I ask thee to apply the blood of Jesus Christ. Lord, we long to be perfectly clean, so that we can come boldly to the throne of grace for more of thee. Thank You Father in Jesus Christ's name.

Amen

General Requirements

Forgiving Spirit

It is of vital importance that we have a spirit of forgiveness to begin with, before we start our prayer. If not it will stand as a blockage between God and us, and our prayers cannot pass that blockage. There must be nothing between our soul and the Savior. We must ask the Father, in the name of Jesus Christ, to remove all blockages of sin so that our prayers can go through to the Father (Matthew 6:14). Let us ask ourselves some very important questions as we prepare to go to God in prayer.

Is everything okay with the Savior and me?

Is it well with me and others?

Have I forgiven that person the other day, when I ignored, said, or did something that was unpleasant?

God is waiting to hear us say to that person, 'Please forgive me for what I said to you. I did not mean to hurt you.' It does not have to be a long and drawn out conversation, but it needs to be said in love and honesty. We can keep it simple as long as it is sincere. Ask yourself, is there anything that I need to say or do to others in a heart of forgiveness? If all is well we may continue our prayers in faith believing that God will also forgive.

Life's events should not be tit for tat. God expects us to have a healthy attitude towards forgiveness if we are to do His work. Our heart must be clean and trustworthy. Can He depend on you and me?

If we forgive men their trespasses our heavenly Father will also forgive us, but if we will not forgive men their trespasses, neither will our Father forgive our trespasses. There is a saying that is so true. It says 'You will only receive as much as you give'. Some people have a very bad attitude towards others, yet they are the first to complain about the faults of others. Forgiving one another should be an ongoing process in life, because every day we need the forgiveness of others so we too must be ready to do the same. It is a give and take situation. Someone was tired of always having to forgive his neighbor, so he came and asked Jesus if seven times should be enough. Jesus replied and said, seventy times seven, in other words as often as it is necessary, forgiveness should be implemented

Simplicity In Prayer

Matthew 6:5-6

A broken and a contrite heart God will not despise. We need only keep it simple when approaching our heavenly Father. We have nothing to be boastful about, we are all sinners saved by grace. Had it not been for the grace of God we would be forever lost, but thank God who remembered that we are flesh and needed a Savior. We could draw an approach from a little child, who is so innocent and does not hold the grudge of yesterday forever. They will soon make it up with their friends, and begin playing with each other again.

Jesus said when we pray, we should not be like the hypocrites, for they love to pray standing in the synagogues and on the street corners to be seen by men. Because of this they have received their reward in full. He told us that when we pray, we should go into our room, close the door and pray to our Father, then our Father, who sees what is done in secret, will reward us openly.

Some people, like the religious leaders in the Old Testament days, wanted to be seen as holy, and public prayer was one way to get attention. Jesus saw their self-righteous act, and taught that the essence of prayer is not public style but private communication with God. There is a place for public prayer, but to pray only where others will notice you indicates that your real audience is not God, but men.

Humility And Repentance

Luke 18:10-14

We must be humble enough to seek repentance. Jesus spoke this parable of the two men who went up to the temple to pray. One was a Pharisee, and the other a Publican (tax collector*)*. The Pharisees stood and stroked his breast and prayed, 'God, I thank you that I am not like other men; robbers, evil doers, adulterers, or even like this tax collector.' He said, 'I fast twice per week and give a tenth of all I earn'. He was really boasting and making an outward show about what he did, but he was not aware of what he didn't do. He should have realized that this was not all required of him.

To **give lip** service to God is not enough. God desires that both inward acts and outward behavior should speak in agreement.

The tax collector stood at a distance. He would not even look up to heaven, but beat his breast and said, 'God have mercy on me a sinner'. Jesus looked on both of these men. He was pleased with the prayers of the tax collector. He asked God to show mercy on him. He saw his unworthiness, and the need to be pardoned by a merciful God. It is His mercy why we are not consumed in our sins, so let us appreciate the mercies of the Lord and give Him thanks. I tell you that this man rather than the other went home justified by God. For everyone who exalts himself will be humbled, and he who humbles himself will be exalted.

Having a humble heart towards God and man is one important element that would generate an answer to our prayers. Humility stems away from being proud or boastful, it should not be so, but one must have a heart filled with loving kindness and compassion for one another. God will not walk with the proud and the scornful; He sees the proud afar off. They have no fellowship with Him until they repent and ask forgiveness for their proud heart. God sees the proud afar off (Matthew 6: 5-6).

Unity Of Believers

Matthew 18:10-20

It is the Holy Spirit's role to unite believers. He leads but we have to be willing to be lead, and to do our part to keep the peace. We will be able to do so by focusing on God, and not on ourselves (see John 3:6, Ephesians 1:13-14, and Acts 1:5). As believers in Christ we belong to one body, unified, and come under one head, Christ Himself, according to 1 Corinthians 12:12. Each member has a God-given ability that can strengthen the whole body. Our special gift, whether small or large, is useful in God's service. As we grow together we will recognize our special area of service.

Accord and unity are vital to the fellowship of Christians. Disunity among believers in churches will cause them to experience division and other problems that will lead to envy, rivalry, selfishness and conceit. The word of God has the unique remedy suggested to fulfill in joy, it is the love that was shed abroad in our hearts that will produce the Christian character. It will quicken us to live in harmony and imbue us with a pattern for personal relationships.

It will make unity more edifying. It will attribute to like-mindedness, people will not think of themselves more highly than they ought to, but they will experience the love that is revealed in Christ, the love that is poured in our hearts by the Holy Spirit.

We are admonished to be kind one to another, tenderhearted, forgiving one another, even as Christ has forgiven you (Ephesians 4:32).

To maintain harmony and unity among believers is so important. It should leave no place for jealousy, anger, and feeling bitter, but our focus should be steadfast, we should keep in mind that Christ is the source and model for our lives. He has provided enough grace to enable us to put off the old life and to put on His righteousness. When believers unite in prayer it can make a great difference in the world in which we live, the people of the world will take notice of our love and want to experience the Christ in whom we believe.

When all believers gather together in oneness, prayer, and faith, great things can happen. The believers, who came together in the days of the Acts of the Apostles had a wonderful experience. They established a sense of togetherness in their coming when they met. The forces of unity was so strong that when they had prayed, the place was shaken where they were assembled, and they were all filled with the Holy Ghost and they spoke the word of God in boldness.

The Word of God states that where two of you on earth agree about anything you ask, it will be done by your Father in heaven, for where two or three come together in His name, there He is with them. It is good and beautiful when believers dwell together in unity. United we stand, but separated we will certainly fall. Let us keep our fellowship tight that the enemy cannot find any place to creep in and spoil God's plans for our lives.

Jesus looked ahead to a new day when He would be present with His followers not in body, but through His Holy Spirit. In the body of believers (the church), the sincere agreement of two people is more powerful than the superficial agreement of thousands, because Christ's Holy Spirit is with them. Two or more believers, filled with the Holy Spirit, will pray according to God's will, not their own, thus their request will be granted (Matthew 18:1920).

Tenacity In Prayer

Luke 18:1-8

Jesus gave a parable. He said supposing a man called on a friend late at night to borrow a loaf of bread for a friend that came unexpectedly to him. Although it is late at night, and perhaps the family have gone to bed, because the friend keeps knocking, the householder will get up and give him what he came for, even if just to get rid of him. He will rise and give him as much as he wants, because of his continuous knocking. We prevail with men but it is not so with God, He is pleased with our asking. This lesson shows us how we should be in prayer. We should go to God in the name of Jesus Christ with boldness and confidence, asking Him for what we need, just as a man does to his neighbor, or friend, who he knows and loves him and wants to help him out.

We must come to God on behalf of others and ourselves. The man did not come for bread for himself, but for the friend. Although we are encouraged to be persistent in prayer and not to give up, it does not mean endless repetitive or painfully long prayer sessions. Always praying means keeping our requests constant before God as we live for Him day by day, believing that he will answer. When we live by faith, we are not to give up, we will develop a spirit of patience to wait until the answer comes. God may delay answering, but His delays always have good reasons. As we persist in prayer we are growing in character, faith, and hope. If unjust judges respond to constant pressure, how much more will a great and loving God respond to us. Since we know that He loves us, we can be confident that He will hear our cries for help (Luke 18:1-18).

Importunity In Prayer

Luke 11:5-8

Jesus gave us a parable of the importance of persistency. He gave us an instance of an honest cause that came to the hearing of an unjust judge. We see that the bad character of the judge who neither feared God or man, did not render him incapable of granting a good request. He had no regard to godliness or honor. He was not doing well with his power, but causing danger and hurt to the people. He had no compassion for people; he was feeling lofty with pride and false power.

Yet he responded rightfully to a poor widow came to him and made application from day to day, crying 'Avenge me of mine adversary that is doing me injustice'. She was feeling helpless and powerless before him.

In the Old Testament days a magistrate is particularly warned not to do wrong to widows and the fatherless, but to plead for widows. However this widow was met with discouragement from this judge because he would not for a while listen to her case. He did not give her notice because she had no bribe to give him, because she was so poor.

The woman had enough faith and persistency to continue worrying this unjust judge with her need for justice. When the judge finally responded to her, he said 'because this widow troubles me I will attend to her case, and do her justice, lest she clamor and weary me.' For she decided that she will give him no rest till it is done. She wrestled in her faith like Jacob of old when he was desperate to be blessed by the angel. Jacob had said, 'I will not let go until you bless me. I am determined, not to let go, I need a blessing, and a blessing I will get', so he held on.

The widow got justice by her continual craving. The persistency of the widow woman moved the unjust judge to act, although he had no intention to do so. God's servants must likewise persist in prayer. God, who is righteous, will respond in answer to our prayer and cause justice to be done. This is a good example to develop a determination not to quit until we get answer to our prayers.

How much more our heavenly Father deals with His children when they bring cases to him? *How hungry and thirsty can you get? How desperate are you to be blessed? Pray, pray, pray.*

Intensity

Matthew 7:7-11

The intensity of the nature of our prayer will determine on how urgent and desperate our need is for what we are praying about. Jesus gave a precept on what we should know when He said to 'Ask, seek, knock'. That is like another way to say 'Pray, pray, pray'. Ask as a beggar asks for alms. Ask as a traveler asks the way. When we ask in faith and lift our burdens to God, He is pleased. So to pray is to enquire of God for the way.

We should seek in prayer like we would seek for something that is of great value, like a precious thing that we have lost, like Daniel in Daniel 9:30.

We should be like the woman who loses one of her precious coins, then lights a candle and searches the house intensely until she finds it. We should knock with holy passion if we desire to enter the house. It is of great importance that we must enter the house, because sin has locked and barred the door against us. But by prayer we can knock, and cry, 'Lord, Lord open to us.' Christ allows us to knock at His door; this is a favor that is not allowed to beggars.

Seeking and knocking implies something more than asking and praying. We must not only ask but we must seek. As we come to God's door we must ask importunately, and not only pray, but plead and wrestle with God.

Jesus tells us to be persistent in persuading God. People often give up after a few half-hearted efforts and conclude that God cannot be found. But knowing God, takes faith, focus, and follow-ups, and Jesus assures us that we will be rewarded. Don't give up in your efforts to seek God. Continue to ask Him for knowledge, patience, wisdom, love, and understanding. The child in Jesus' examples asked his father for bread and fish, good and necessary items. If the child had asked for poisonous snakes, would the wise father have granted his request? Sometimes God knows we are praying for 'snakes' and does not give us what we ask for, even though we persist in our prayers.

As we learn know to God better as a loving father, we learn to ask for what is good for us, and then He grants it. Christ is showing us the heart of God the Father. God is not selfish, begrudging, or stingy, and we don't have to beg or grovel as we come with our requests. He is a loving Father who understands, cares, and comforts. If humans can be kind, imagine how God, the Creator of kindness, can be (Matthew 7: 7-11).

Jesus said, 'Therefore I tell you, whatever you ask for in prayer, believe that you will receive it, and it shall be ours.' Jesus prayed to His Father that His will would be done. Our prayers are often motivated by our own interests and desires but we should remember that 'whatever' does not mean that we can have all that we asked for all the time. We should note how Jesus prayed. He prayed with the will of His Father's interest in mind. We should check on ourselves to see if our prayers are focus on our interest or on God's. Prayer should be prayed in faith. Therefore, faith is acting out of what we believe. It is the practical expression of the confidence that I have in God's word. It is spending time to read and meditate on the word, listening to what God is saying to me in anticipation, and getting ready to put it in action (Matthew 11:24).

Confidence And Expectation

Matthew 11:24

We know that we have confidence that whatever we ask in His name, that He will give it. When we have knowledge of the integrity of a person's character, and we ask for something from them, our knowledge gives us an assurance to ask and believe that we will receive it. It is the same with our heavenly Father. He said, 'If we should ask anything in His name He will give it to us.' He says we often don't receive because we don't ask according to His will. He will not withhold anything from those who walk uprightly. Jesus said, 'Ask and it will be given, seek and we will find, knock and the door will be opened.' We should ask in faith and expectation, that we will be granted our request (Mathew 21:22).

When we are asking for anything, we must remember that our asking must be in His name and be according to God's character and will. We cannot use His name as a magic formula to fulfill our selfish desires. If we are sincerely and faithful to God, in our asking and line up with His will, our prayers will be answered (John 14:14).

Have you been pressured by expectations?

Do you feel that too many people are depending on you with their expectations? This can be over-taxing on your schedules. Do they expect you to 'do this', 'be there', 'find that', and 'make that call'? It would seem that everyone wants something from you while they themselves are not prepared to pull their weight. The family, the school committee, the club, community, ladies department, the whole lot has been left on you to give.

Try not to get burnt out because of the expectation of others. So many times we feel so disappointed because we ask amiss, not in faith. The Bible says without faith it is impossible to get anything from God.

Readers, we cannot afford to waver when praying to God in faith, believing. Suppose there was an urgent need that required God to intervene, and we found out that we did not get an answer because we did not ask in faith. How would you feel? I know that we are all guilty over this one because our faith does not always stand tall; it is a fault on our part. But we don't have to live this way, we can cry out God to increase our faith that we can be more confident in our expectations to receive what we ask from Him.

Without Many Words

Matthew 6:7

Jesus said that we are not to pray using the same words repeatedly. It is no way to believe that God will answer our prayers. Jesus encourages us to pray persistent prayers. He condemns the shallow repetition of words. We can never pray too much, but our prayers must be in faith, honesty, and in sincerity. We should pray, but really mean what we pray about. Matthew 6:7 shows that we do not always have to pray long prayers. Some people pray like the tax collector, in a few words but insincere or self-gloating.

Every person has the right to pray to God in the name of Jesus, whatever way they can. Our Father knows best, but He still waits to hear from us. Sometimes our prayers can be without words: it could be a sigh, other times it maybe a groan, or a tear, or a look upwards. Thank

God for the Holy Spirit who know all the signals of our needs, and what it means. He helps us in praying to the Father.

Sometimes we pray using fewer words, not because we do not know what to pray for, but because the burden may seem so heavy that our mouths cannot express it in words. Nevertheless the Holy Spirit, our Comforter, is right by our side to help us pray with words that we cannot uttered. Yes, we groan at times, we cry at times but God understands each groan of His children. Just as in the example of a loving attentive mother who knows and understands the cry and groans of her young child, so our loving Father stands to listen when we are not able to pray aloud. Some of the times we are able to cry aloud, other times we cannot but deeply groan, as to say, 'Lord help me. 'O Lord, come to my rescue and deliver me from all evil, for thou art the kingdom, the power and the glory.' *Thank you Lord.*

Unceasingly

1 Thessalonians 5:17

Praying continually without ceasing is a command from the Lord. The believer is called to a life of prayer; to neglect this is an act of disobedience. The obligation to pray is a lifelong and absolute necessity. When all is going well, it is sometimes difficult to remember to pray, but it can be easier to pray when we are experiencing problems. Problems will drive us to our knees to seek the Lord for intervention. Praying without ceasing will result in maturity, a combination of time and mistake. It takes time to get to maturity; it is a long process with trials on every side but with God on our side it will be worth it all.

Along life's journey we will experience a lot of mistakes and pitfalls while growing into maturity, but mistakes are learning processes that give good rewards if we use each one as a learning tool. So it is time to pray without ceasing and sign up in the 'school of maturity'. As we must continue to eat, sleep, and breathe to stay alive, so it is imperative that we must continue in a program of prayer to stay alive spiritually. Sometimes the physical body needs drastic action to get going again, such as an electric shock or artificial respiration. Likewise, sometimes we need an extra spiritual boost to get our prayer life revived and back on track, with more steadfastness and intensity.

I don't know about you, but sometimes my prayer barrel gets low. When I realize this, I make all effort to be filled up again to pray, until I pray. For the child of God, he can cry out to the Father, and He will be right there, to lift up and carry us until we are able to stand. Isn't it so amazing how our Father does not give up on us when we are experiencing emptiness and feelings of despair? He urges our spirit to pray, and pray again. I could not go on without Him. Life would be one big mess, but thank God for Jesus Christ who pleaded my cause, and yours. The word of God admonishes us to pray without ceasing, to develop a lifestyle of prayer.

Not Knowing How To Pray:

Firstly, we cannot foresee the future. We pray for the development of our desired lifestyle, for example, when Israel rejected God as king and prayed and got a king it did not need. He was short-lived because of his disobedience. God was not interested in his sacrifice and burnt offering; He would rather a broken and a contrite heart (1 Samuel 15:22, 23). What a blessed experience of grace when we can pray every day, 'Thy will be done.'

Secondly, we do not know what is best for us. Man proposes, God disposes. 'The steps of a good man are ordered by the Lord'. Then He will offer absolute assurance that an answer to our petition is forthcoming.

Thirdly, when we are involved in spiritual warfare, we cannot always understand the workings of the Spirit. There are times when a Christian is seized with burdens which are beyond his understanding, and consequently are beyond his ability to state them, thus he groans in the spirit because there is no way to say in words what his soul is feeling, but thank God for the blessed Holy Spirit who so lovingly takes our groaning to the Father.

Join me in prayer.

Father, I come to You in the name of Jesus. I bring the sacrifice of praise, thanksgiving and adoration. Father, I thank You for the spirit of forgiveness so that I can freely forgive. Help me to constantly read Your words on matters on how to keep my heart glowing with grace and compassion for others. Father, I believe that You are able to do exceeding above that I may ask or think.

Thank You for the work of the Holy Spirit in our prayer life when we do not know how to pray, or what I should pray.

I thank You for the blood of Jesus Christ that was shed on Calvary. Thank You for Jesus Christ, Your beloved Son. I believe that He died and rose again, and He is now seated at Your right hand making intercession for us. Thank you. I confess that Jesus Christ is Lord of my life.

I pray for unity among my brothers and sisters in the Lord that peace may abound more and more. I pray for ministers of the gospel, for government, and for the unsaved, that You will draw them by Your Spirit.

Father, Your word declares that no man can come to You unless he is drawn by Your Spirit, so Father God I ask You in the name of Jesus Christ to do a drawing so that men can be saved.

Thank You for doing so in Jesus Christ's name.

Amen

10

Answers Refused Because Of:

SIN:

S in is transgression of God's law, says Romans 6:1. We are all guilty of sin; the Jew, the Gentile and the pagan have all sinned. In both the In both the Old and the New Testament we have interesting vocabularies for the various forms of sin.

To show how important a fact of human life sin is, let us have a look at the different ways it is presented in our lives.

1 **Falling short of the glory of God:** also missing the mark (Romans 3:23).

2 **Unrighteousness, iniquity:** the basic meaning of these words is 'injustice' or 'dishonesty' (1 John 1:9).

3 **Trespass**: as stated in the 'Lord's Prayer'. It means to have fallen, when we should have resisted a temptation, or maintained a spiritual walk (James 5:17).

4 **Iniquity:** as in lawlessness (1 John 3:4).

5 **Transgression:** it is irreligion in general, like the Atheist who chooses to live in rebellion against God, and godly standards (Jude 1:14).

6 **Debt**: accursed in the sense of Matthew's version in the Lord's Prayer, forgive our debts, as we forgive others. Debts are what we owe to God for our sins (Matthew 6:12).

7 **Disobedience:** shows how sin entered our world by one man's disobedience. The root idea is to neglect to hear and heed God's command (Romans 5:19).

We cannot use ignorance as an excuse; we can fit in the promise in 1 John 1:7, that the blood of Jesus Christ will cleanse us from all our sins.

In Psalm 66:18, it states that if we regard iniquity in our hearts the Lord will not hear us when we pray. Our confession of sin must be continuous, because we have a tendency to continue to do wrong. But true confession requires us to listen to God and stop doing what is wrong. David confessed his sin and prayed, 'Forgive my hidden faults. Keep your servant from willful sins'. When we refuse to repent about our sins we place a wall between God and us. We may not remember every sin that we have ever committed but our attitude should be one of confession, obedience, and repentance. When people are purged from their sin, there is great relief and hope. No matter how difficult our experience is, we can look forward to the day of celebrating when God will completely restore us.

Sin makes one feel ugly. It is distasteful, feels terrible and has bad consequences. Sin will bar us from God's door for evermore. Sin is also lawlessness, it is anything that is contrary to what the word of God commands, or forbids. All unrighteousness is sin.

Sin will stop us from getting along with others. It will always show up something different from what one expects. We must stop from sinning for it will stop us from loving. Sin wants us dead. Sin is a hard paymaster. It pays the right wages, nothing less, the wages of sin is death, but the gift of God is eternal life through Jesus Christ our Lord. The good news is that the blood of Jesus Christ cleanses us from all sin (1 John 1:17).

Sin is the cause of fear, which is like a dark shadow that envelopes us. Fear will ultimately imprison us within ourselves. Each of us has at some time or another been imprisoned by fear: fear of rejection, uncertainties, sickness, or even death. But we can conquer fear by the bright, liberating lights of the Lord who brings salvation. If we want to dispel the darkness of fear, let us remember to pray that 'the Lord is my light and my salvation, whom shall we fear' (Psalms 27:1).

A healthy fear is the fear of the Lord, which means to show deep respect and honor to Him. We should demonstrate true reverence by our humble attitude and genuine worship.

Selfishness

James 4:3

We cannot expect to retain a spirit of selfishness and expect God to be faithful to us. We must reach out to others and be caring and sharing, that in time to come someone will reach out to us also. It should be no longer me, I, and I; rather it should be all of us. Our selfish attitude should never be allowed to continue once we have identified it. Christ Jesus was willing to give His life for others, even for the people who put Him to death.

James 4:3 states that we ask and we do not receive because we ask with wrong motives, that we may spend what we ask for on our own pleasures. We should not seek God's approval for what we have already planned to do. Our prayers will become powerful if we allow God to change our desires so that they perfectly correspond with His will for our lives (1 John 3: 21).

Selfishness will lead to blind ambitions (Judges 9:2-5). It will keep us from being sensitive to the weaknesses of others (Proverbs 2:20). It will cause us to use God's gift for selfish purposes. Selfishness can be cured by servant-hood (Philippians 2:3).

Selfish ambition can ruin a church, but genuine humility can build it. When one is humble he or she will have a true prospective about others (Romans 12:3). This does not mean that we should put ourselves down, because before God we are all sinners saved only by God's grace. We are saved and receive great worth in God's kingdom, therefore we are urged to lay aside selfishness, and treat others with respect and common courtesy, and consider the interest of others as more important than our own.

Many people live to make a good impression about themselves, but selfish ambition is vain deceit, it will only bring discord. Let us, with God's help, acknowledge selfishness in our own lives and pray for forgiveness.

Doubt

James 1:5-7

James again stated that if anyone lacks wisdom they should ask God, who gives generously to all. When we ask we must believe without doubting, because if we doubt we will be like the wave of the sea, blown and tossed by the wind. A double-minded person is unstable in all his ways and will not receive anything from the Lord. James was not talking only about knowledge but about the ability to make wise decisions in different circumstances. Whosoever needs to have more wisdom should pray to God, and He will generously supply us with what we ask for. We have no need to grope in the dark hoping to stumble on answers; we should ask God for guidance to make choices.

It takes wisdom to exercise practical discernment. It begins with respect for God that leads to right living and results in increased ability to tell what is right from wrong. God is willing to give us this wisdom, but we will be unable to receive it if our goals are self-centered instead of God-centered. To learn God's will, we need to read His word and ask Him to show us how to obey it, then we must do what He tells us.

Even among God's chosen people in the Old Testament we read about those who doubted.

Abraham doubted when God told him he would be a father in his old age (Genesis 17:13).

Sarah doubted when she heard that she would be a mother in old age (Genesis 18:12).

Moses doubted when God told him to return to Egypt to be the leader of the people (Exodus 3:10-15).

The Israelites doubted when they faced difficulties in the desert (Exodus 16:1-3).

Zachariah doubted when he was told that he would be a father in his old age (Luke 1:18).

Gideon doubted when he was told that he would be a judge and leader (Judges 6:14-23).

Thomas doubted when he heard that Jesus was raised from the dead (John 20:24-25).

We can add the times when we have doubted in one way or another, but now we have developed the right attitude to trust God no matter what.

Disobedience

Proverbs 28:9

Disobedience is a sin according to Genesis 3:14-19. It hurts others around us according to Exodus 8:15. It will make our lives more difficult, warns Deuteronomy 2:14-15.

God will not listen to our prayers if we harbor intent to go back to our sin as soon as we get off our knees. If we want to forsake our sin and follow Him, He will willingly listen, no matter how bad our sin has been. What closes the ears of God is not the depth of our sin, but our secret intention to do it again. The sin of disobedience is as cruel as the sin of witchcraft. If we are willing and obedient we will eat the good of the land.

It is never healthy to act in the spirit of disobedience, even when dealing with our earthly parents, much less our heavenly Father. The penalty is very serious if this act is allowed to continue in one's life. To obey what God says is better than making a sacrifice. The sin of disobedience is like the sin of witchcraft. Let's obey God in words and deeds; it will be beneficial in years to come. Some people are reaping what they sow today, because they chose to disobey or because they chose to obey.

Inhumanity

Proverbs 21:13

If a man shuts his ears to the cry of the poor, he too will cry out and not be answered. We should work to meet the needs of the poor and protect their rights. One day we may be in need of such services ourselves. Life is like a merry go round, as it goes around we will meet others on our journey.

Let us be careful how we treat the people we meet each day. We must be mindful that everyone has an opportunity to apply to the blood of Jesus to receive salvation, therefore we are all applicants standing at the foot of the cross. Hallelujah! The ground is level; we don't have to be trampling on each other to get to the Savior. He knows us as individuals, He is interested in all our affairs, His hand is still stretched out calling to His children to come to Him, all who labor and are heavy laden. He said that His yoke is easy and His burden is light. We must do the work of His kingdom and prepare for His return. Jesus also told us how to prepare for life in His eternal kingdom by living a life to please Him now. We should be willing to show mercy to the merciless, because one day we might be in need of mercy. Jesus said, 'Blessed are the merciful for they shall obtain mercy' (Luke 18:11).

We can measure how much we love God by how well we treat others. Jesus' example of giving a cup of cold water to a thirsty child is a good model of unselfish service. A child usually cannot return a favor, so every good deed that we do, let's do to others as if we are the one that is receiving it (Matthew 10:42).

Christianity is not for people who think that they are already good; it is for people who know that they have failed and want help (Matthew 9:9-13, Luke 5:27).

Join me in prayer.

Praise the Lord, thank You Jesus, Hallelujah. Father, I come to You in the name of Jesus Christ, thank You for redeeming my life from destruction. I now receive cleansing through the shed blood of Jesus Christ, Your Son. Father, grant me a holy thirst for Your words that water cannot quench. Father, I long to be lost in You. O Lord, I give You my heart, I give You my soul and all that is within me.

Holy Father, I thank You for transformation. Truly Father, it has wrought newness of life so that I can now have sweet fellowship with You and Your Son Jesus. My God, please help me to walk in that newness of life; O Father, my desire is to allow Your will to be done in my life, please lead me into all truth.

I ask of You to remember the family of God, the brethren. Father, You know their struggles to make it through this troubled time. Please Father, let Your Holy Spirit keep reminding them of the hope that they have in You.

Lord, I just thank You for that hope that those who put their trust in You have; they will never be ashamed. Lord, we thank You. I ask these mercies in Jesus Christ's name.

Amen

11

Hinderances To Prayer

Galatians 5:19

There are hindrances that prevent our prayers from be answered; we have to do all that lies in our power to remove those blockages. God is willing and ready to help us move the hindrances, if we ask Him in faith, He will. Jesus came to destroy all sin, and hindrances from our lives, so don't take it lying down without a fight to keep our victory over the enemy. Having lived in the former life of flesh, it is imperative that we guard against the works of the flesh from warring against our spirit. The enemy will try to creep back if we fail to plan, and maintain a successful prayer life.

When the believer becomes one with Christ, a wonderful transformation takes place. We no longer live according to the pattern of the world, but we become new creatures. The word of God declares that we should mortify the deeds of the flesh, meaning to 'kill off' the flesh. The old works of the flesh must be crucified daily (you can find a list of the works of the flesh in Galatians 5:19-22).

It is of vital importance that we keep on top of things, by taking heed to the word of God, and praying without ceasing. See to it that all loopholes that could possibly lead to a life of sin are kept closed. The devil does not have a key to your heart. He may want to come in when you least expect but he has no access without your consent. The believer is expected to walk in the Spirit, and the lust of the flesh will not be able to creep back into our thoughts, deeds, or actions when they choose to. The enemy of our soul is always looking for an invitation to visit, as long as he sees an opportunity he will not hesitate, he will move in without warming. *So watch out!*

We will not dwell too long on dealing with these negative actions but it is necessary to know them and the dangers of living with them. Our bodies are the temple of God; therefore they shall not seek residence in God's temple. Should they show up at any given time, we should establish the truth that they are not welcomed to stay, you are under new management. We must take into account that the Holy Spirit is in control of the believer. Jesus will satisfy your soul, there should be no more lusting for the things of this world. Let us agree in prayer and denounce this deadly behavior that hinders our progress.

Father, in the all-powerful name of Jesus Christ we cancel these activities from operating in our lives. We take a stand and erase each one of these fleshy vices with the blood of Jesus Christ. Thank You, in Jesus Christ's name, Amen.

Adultery

Adultery is being unfaithful to one's spouse by having sexual intercourse with someone else. There is another sort of adultery; when a man looks on woman in a lustful way in his heart. The word of God says, 'I tell you that anyone who looks at a woman lustfully has already committed adultery' (Matthew 5:28).

Jesus insisted that purity of heart among those who follow Him is more important than laws that people could not obey. What has often started as lust of the eye can lead to adultery and murder. We need to build a right relationship with God and ask Him for help to avoid living our lives with this sin. We can ask God to help us to overcome and change our behavior. If we draw near to God He will help to disarm these vices from operating in our lives.

There is nothing too hard for God. God's forgiveness reached out to the woman who was caught in the very act of adultery. God's grace is sufficient to keep us from committing adultery. We may ask, 'How can I be perfect in character?' In this life we cannot be flawless, but we can aspire to be as like Christ as possible. We can separate ourselves from the world's sinful values. We are to be devoted to God's desire rather than our own. We can ask God to change us from inside that we may have a different behavior, and grow to maturity. Our tendency to sin must never deter us from striving to be more like Christ.

Father, in the name of Jesus Christ I denounce this deadly activity of adultery in the lives of the readers of this book. Lord Jesus Christ grant them the strength to be made whole in the inner man. Father, we claim complete deliverance over this sin in Jesus' mighty name, Amen.

Fornication

Fornication is sexual relation by mutual agreement between two persons not married to each other. The biblical term is not limited to promiscuous sexual conduct between single people only. The Bible speaks of fornication in a general way, whether committed by single or by married persons, but it also uses the term 'adultery'. It is an act between an unmarried man, and unmarried woman. Sexual immorality is a temptation that is always before us. In movies and television, sex outside marriage is treated as a normal, even desirable part of life, while marriage is often shown as confining and joyless. We can even be looked down on by others if we are suspected of being pure. But God does not forbid sexual sin just to be difficult. He knows its power to destroy us physically and spiritually. We should never underestimate the power of sexual immorality.

The sin of fornication has devastated countless lives and destroyed families, churches, communities, and even nations. God wants to protect us from damaging ourselves and others, and so He offers to fill our loneliness and our desires with Himself. He will grant us the necessary help that we need to live clean lives. God's grace is sufficient to keep us from continuing a life of fornication. Let us take all the members of our bodies and ask Him to purge and cleanse and purify them for His use, in Jesus Christ's name.

Father, in Jesus' powerful name we claim deliverance over the spirit of fornication. Help us to be always aware that our bodies are the temple of the Living God. We ask for strength to overcome this practice of fornication, thank You Father, in Jesus Christ's name. Amen.

Uncleanness

Uncleanness or impurity refers to lewdness of thoughts, speech, and behavior, and sexual impurity. The off-color jokes, the flirtatious gestures, the mental savoring of suggestive words or lustful images, any behavior or filthy thoughts, all add up to uncleanness. Immorality springs from the thoughts of our mind and the intent of the heart. The practice of uncleanness is a sin of the flesh that is hidden deep within the mind; they can fester and develop in prostitution and in other works of the flesh.

Paul urged the believers that there must not be even a hint of sexual immorality, or any kind of impurity, or greed, because these are improper for God's holy people. Neither should there be obscenity, foolish talk or coarse joking which are out of place (Ephesians 5:3).

Jesus gave Himself for us, an offering and a sacrifice to God, for a sweet smelling aroma. But fornication and all uncleanness, or covetousness, let it not once be named among you as fitting as saints.

Colossians 6:35 speaks of mortifying our members against uncleanness. Paul urges us to consider ourselves dead and unresponsive to sexual immorality, impurity, lust, evil desires and greed. It is just like a limb that is diseased on a tree, so these practices must be cut off before they destroy the whole tree. We must make a conscious, daily decision to remove anything that supports or feed these desires, and to rely on the Holy Spirit to empower us to live right.

Father, I claim victory through the blood of Jesus Christ over the spirit of uncleanness, in Jesus Christ's mighty name, Amen.

Lasciviousness

Lasciviousness is sexual excess, shameless conduct of any kind. It also means wantonness in sexual relations. It is the self-asserting propensity indulged without check or regard to ordinary propriety, especially in libidinous gratification. It also refers to the willingness to indulge in any form of pleasure. We should take responsibility to restrain ourselves from the indulgence in this ungodly behavior.

Father, we come to You in the all-powerful name of Jesus Christ, and claim deliverance over the sin of lasciviousness. Thank You for cleansing us from this sin, in Jesus Christ's name. Amen.

Idolatry

Idolatry is the worship of idols or anything that is worshipped instead of God. In our modern world idolatry is no longer as visible as when people worshipped the golden calf, but it can be seen in the exaltation of human desire above the law of God. Paul used this incident in scripture from Exodus 32:4 showing that idolatry, immorality, and grumbling before God are all temptations that still face Christians.

This behavior can be only overcome by God's strength. In the time of Moses, the people used objects that they made to create worship, but true worship of the living God cannot be created, worship is bred from hearts willing to submit to the Holy Spirit. Some people will choose to worship anything, even their children, money, profession and material gains, rather than worshipping the true and living God. We were made to worship God so if we do not worship Him, there will remain an empty vacuum that will lead us to worship as in the sin of idolatry, which is connected to pagan religion. Some people will also choose to worship anything other than the true and living God, gods that cannot see or hear. They will shape a god and carve an idol, which does not profit them anything. We often think of an idol as a statue made of wood or stones, but in reality an idol is anything natural that is given sacred value and power. They cannot see or hear and do not have feelings.

Father, help us not to have or worship any other gods beside You, who are the true and

Living God, as beside You there is no other. Father, we give You glory and praise Your name for Your great power over the universe, and over all flesh, in Jesus Christ's name. Amen.

Witchcraft

Witchcraft is sorcery, the tampering with evil powers, dabbling in the occult and witches. It relates to a Greek word that originally denoted use of drugs, and also refers to the employment of magic, sorcery and the black arts in general. The child of God should not take part in this wicked practice. We are no more under the law of sin, but we are now under grace. We have no need to return to the beggarly elements of satanic devices.

God had forbidden Israel to have anything to do with witchcraft, divination, sorcery, and mediums (Deuteronomy 18:19) and in those days the people who practiced these sins were put to death (Exodus 22:18). Oftentimes people who practiced the occult in the name of pagan gods would return to the occult when they could not hear from God.

Those who practice such sins have Satan and demons as the source of their information. God will not reveal His will to them. He always speaks from His word, the Bible (2 Samuel 28:28).

In the name of Jesus Christ we come against the spirit of witchcraft. You have no power over the people of God. We plead the powerful blood of Jesus Christ over this spirit of witchcraft, and cancel its activity and render it helpless in Jesus Christ's name. Father, we confess that You are our God and have power over the powers of evil. Jesus, You came to destroy all that the devil has done. In Jesus Christ's name. Amen.

Hatred

Hatred is when one holds a grudge against others with or without a cause. It is the opposite of love and the tool of our archenemy, Satan.

We can ask God for a heart of love and understanding, to change our behavior to love even our enemies. At every instance when strong feelings of anger or hatred is held onto, no matter how hard the person tries to pretend or adopt a certain pose, whether or not his or her face shows it, there will be a very unpleasant and hostile vibration that other people can sense.

Even animals can sense this vibration from a person who is full of hatred; they too can sense when an angry attitude is present. Hatred is compared to an enemy, an internal enemy; it has no other function than to cause harm. When hatred is dwelling in the heart of a person it will demonstrate itself in his or her behavior.

Hatred has no purpose other than to destroy us. To resolve any anger that may give rise to a feeling of hatred we should take the opportunity to settle it as quickly as possible. It is important to understand that anger will destroy our happiness. It is not possible to simply suppress anger and hatred. It can only be eradicated by the blood of Jesus.

Father, You have not given us the spirit of anger, or hatred, but a spirit of love and a sound mind. Heavenly Father, we ask You for strength to overcome this sin of hatred that wants to control our lives. Please root out hatred and the close relatives of anger now with the blood of Jesus. Lord, help us to love even our enemies, in Jesus Christ's name. Amen.

Variance

Variance is strife or discord and disagreement between people. It prevents harmony. We do not need to live our lives in this bondage by having discord among ourselves and others. There is a better way to enjoy freedom from worry: a life of peace and harmony with everyone. We must understand that contention is like a fire, it will burn up all that is good. It will put families and society into a flame. We should take great care to prevent quarrels among relatives and those that are under special regulations to each other (Proverbs 25:22).

By allowing the word of God to dwell richly in our heart, we will create true and lasting harmony. Colossians 3:13 instructs us that if anyone has a complaint against another, even as Christ forgave you, so you also must do.

Lord, help us to be kind and forgiving, grant us a heart like Yours. Father, I thank you for the power to live at peace and in unity with everyone. Purify our hearts with the blood of Jesus that we may maintain the peace that surpasses all understanding. I ask this in Jesus Christ's name. Amen.

Emulation

Emulation is jealousy or envy, or to grudge others. The spirit of jealousy and envy are closely related, they act out in improper ways, like suspects of others without adequate cause. An envious person discontentedly desires and covets the good and attainments of others. It includes sighing, groaning or complaining against another brother or sister in

Christ. It is altogether too easy to blame others for our problems in times of hardship. When we feel helpless to change circumstances, we can feel frustration against those closest to us. It is said that jealousy is as cruel as the grave. The wrong kind of jealousy can bring a person to a point where he sins against God, as did the 10 half brothers of Joseph (Genesis 37:11). There is no need to envy or grudge others for what they possess. Life can be sought by planning and focus on not what others have but what we can afford until we can get more. It is best to be contented with what we have. We can ask God for an increase rather than to keep coveting others.

Father, we pray for a contented spirit, we make a command over this evil spirit of emulation to take its flight. It has no place in the lives of Your people. In Jesus Christ's name. Amen

Wrath

Wrath refers to heated anger. It is the anger of men mainly in disagreement to one another. It has to do with out bursts of anger and hostility. Wrath goes beyond anger and is associated with vengeance or rage. It has been described as having a roaring furnace of indignation within. When wrath cools, it leaves residue of viciousness. A bad feeling continues within even when the boiling, seething wrath disappears. Some people would rather live in wrath than to live in a life of peace.

Arrogance and pride will keep a person from returning to God because arrogance acknowledges no need for help from any human or from God. It is like pride, it will intensify all other sins, because we see no need to repent and to give up pride. Persistent sinning will harden a person's heart, making it difficult to repent. Deliberate choosing to disobey God can scorch the conscience, and each sin makes the next one easier to commit. We should not allow arrogance to make a hard path deep within us. We should steer far away from sinful practices.

Anger has an effect on our spiritual health and what it produces also has a profound effect on our physical organism. It can cause a rise in blood pressure, arterial changes, respiratory trouble, liver upset, and more. Anger and rage and strong emotions have been listed by physicians as attributing to, aggravating and even causing, health issues such as asthma. Rage and anger will upset one's thinking process so that one cannot form a logical conclusion or pass sound judgment.

We should follow good examples when we deal with others as a farmer uses special tools to plant and harvest tender herbs so he will not destroy them. He takes into account how fragile they are in the same way that God takes all our individual concerns and weaknesses in account (Proverbs 14:29, Romans 14:19).

Father God, we plead the blood of Jesus that was shed on the cross against this demon of wrath, we cast it out now and I render it helpless. Father, we declare that the spirit of wrath shall have no dominion over Your people. We pray and declare that peace shall be our portion, in Jesus Christ's name, Amen.

Strife

Strife is having a selfish ambition and denotes wrangling, dissension and disorder.

Strife is encouraged when one hot word begets another; it is like the cutting of a dam: when the water cuts a little passage, it widens the breach and then there is no stopping it. We should take heed of the first spark of contention, and put it out as soon as it happens.

Abraham understood how to deal with brewing strife. Abraham said to Lot, 'Let there be no strife, I pray thee, between me and you, and between my herdsmen and yours. Is not the whole land before you? If you should go to the right I will go to the left.' This resolution between them was rooted in their relationship of togetherness.

In the event of strife one has to be flexible to agreement to prevent further quarrel and misunderstanding between each other. Strife is a deadly enemy weapon; Satan uses this weapon in the lives of believers the most when we are not aware of his tricks. Strife can be seen and heard from afar, it goes on and on, until and beyond death if is not resolved quickly. Strife leaves traces in its track that continues to the next generation. We need to put it out from its roots before it begins to germinate and increase in its roots.

Mighty God, in Jesus Christ's name, we pray for Your help that we may follow peace with all men, through the good and bad times. We pray against strife, we take a stand against the demon of strife; we rebuke and cancel its activities in the name of Jesus Christ. Amen.

Sedition

Sedition is dissensions, rebellious actions and the determination to remain unyielding on wicked grounds. A conflict occurred when both Jacob and Rebecca deceived Isaac. When deception grows in a family and members of a family choose to take sides in a dispute, it brings polarization. It is said that factors in families grow whenever there is a diminished capacity to love each member of the family and seek overall unity. Commitment to each other is destroyed by self-centeredness.

Therefore, sedition is like a weapon with sharp edges that can capture its victims with only a small pull. It is subtle, and works to undermine until it takes the whole area. But don't be caught out by this devastating deception, put on the whole armour of God, that you may not be caught unaware in the paws of the enemy. For God is able to do exceedingly abundantly above whatever we say or think.

Father, we pray in the name of Jesus Christ that You may grant us the spirit of discernment to detect this deadly weapon of sedition. Grant us the power over the spirit of rebellion that it will not have dominion over us or our brothers and sisters in the Lord. Help us to be bold and strong in the power of Your might. This we humbly ask in Jesus Christ's name. Amen.

Heresies

Heresy is permanent, organized divisions or cliques. We are told in the Epistle of 2 Peter that heresy was prevalent in the churches. There was a false prophet that was influencing believers within the church. They were using false doctrine, especially the lust of the flesh, to draw people away from the truth. Peter exhorted the believers that the warfare against heresy cannot be won by debating doctrine, or disapproving heresy. The heart of the problem could be solved if believers gain a genuine knowledge of Christ. After knowing Christ in a personal way the believer will be enlightened to detect the truth from what is false. Some stories become heresies when it is told from one person to another. We must be aware and hear the full truth instead of running with hearsay. Let us keep ourselves from tale bearing; it is deadly and can cause unnecessary problems to our lives.

Holy Father, we take authority and pull down the strong hold of this spirit of heresy from among Your chosen people. Lord my God, in the name of Jesus Christ, help us to occupy our time in the knowledge of Your word, so that we may not waste precious time in heresies. Thank You, we ask this in the name of Jesus Christ. Amen.

Envying

To envy someone is to covet or wish we had what he or she possesses. It goes beyond simply admiring; instead of 'She has a nice ring', for instance, we say in our heart, 'I should have that'. Coveting includes envy and resentment over what others have and you don't.

Envy is ill will and is related to strife among each other. As believers in Christ we should seek eternal peace through Christ; He is the way, the truth, and the life. Each person has a sinful nature that is contrary to God, but we don't have to live in them. We can and must ask God for His forgiveness to stand against the wiles of the devil, who is the author of these sins. Without the saving work of Christ, every person is destined for eternal destruction. But there is hope in the shed blood of Jesus Christ. We have only to ask for forgiveness in faith, then know that we are forgiven and take authority over the spirit of envy.

Anger is another associate of envy; it blinds us of our sins. It makes us miserable, and it can also lead us to other sins such adultery and stealing. Envying others is a useless exercise, because God is able to provide everything we really need. In order to stop envying what others have we need to practice being content with what we have.

If ever you feel envious against someone about their success, try your best and pray to God for the ability to remain in love so that you too can be successful (Exodus 20:17).

In Philippians 4:11 Paul urges believers in 'the significance of contentment', explaining that it is a matter of perspective, so instead of thinking about what we don't have, we should give God thanks for what He has given us and strive to be content. After all, our most important possession is free and available to all, and that is eternal life through Christ. When we are blinded by envy and hatred it is almost impossible to see our own sins (1 Kings 20:21, Deuteronomy 15:21).

Loving Father, we pray for the renewing of our minds with Your love for others, that this spirit of envying may not be found in us. In Jesus Christ's name I pray. Amen.

Murder

Murder is the premeditated killing of another human being. Cain committed the first murder, and from then on the sin of murder was unleashed on the whole world (Genesis 8:4-10). The sin of murder springs from deeply ingrained selfishness, a willingness to sacrifice one's fellowmen for one's own desire or interest. Long before it is it affects the quality of interpersonal relationship while destroying the spiritual life of the perpetrator.

God's creation is sacred to Him. Therefore, when a person takes the life of another human being it destroys someone else who is made in God's image. The sixth commandment says 'Thou shall not commit murder'. God intended for us to respect human life, so we have no God-given right to take away someone else's life. 1 Peter 4:15 states, 'but let none of you suffer as a murderer, a thief, an evildoer, or a busybody in other people's matters'.

We are told in Deuteronomy 5:17 that we are capable of committing murder in our hearts, because it has its roots in anger and hatred (1Kings 21:8). We murder others when we use our tongue to speak evil against others.

Lord, we commit all the members of our body to You for personal cleansing from evil thoughts in order to overcome this dangerous sin of murder. Lord, our behavior and the wrong use of our tongue can be deadly weapons as well, so please give us strength to overcome in Jesus Christ's name. Amen.

Drunkenness

Drunkenness is being overcome and intoxicated by strong drink. Alcohol blurs the individual's mind and gives a false hope, but God is at hand to give deliverance for the asking. Freedom is a mark of Christian faith, freedom from sin and guilt, and freedom to use and enjoy anything that comes from God. But Christians should not abuse this freedom and hurt themselves or others.

Noah was overtaken by drunkenness according to Genesis 9: 20-27. We can easily fall when overcome by strong drink. Consuming strong drinks will not solve our problems; it takes a change of heart and believing that God is able to give us the strength through His word to control this deadly habit of strong drink.

We are responsible for what we put into our bodies in the form of food and drink, knowing that our body is the temple of God. We will have to give account of how we treated God's temple. Sometimes people are plagued with illness because of how they abuse their bodies. The price will be high in the end when it comes to a show in bad health. There are so many people who are experiencing poor health because of a lifetime of abuse of too much of the wrong input in their bodies. We can take heed by not self-inflicting and indulging in the wrong habits.

Drinking too much strong drink will lead to alcoholism, and gluttony leads to obesity. Be careful that what God has allowed you to enjoy doesn't develop into a bad habit that controls you. We should not be drunken with strong drink, but rather be filled with God's word and stay sober, be vigilant and be aware of Satan who is the manager behind all these unlawful activities of the flesh.

Father, we come to You in the name of Your Son Jesus. We ask that the Holy Spirit will help us not to indulge in alcoholic behavior that plagues the lives of so many people. Father God, we make a command against the spirit of drunkenness that results from excess of strong drinks, in Jesus Christ's name. Amen.

Reveling

Reveling is excessive eating or gluttony or carousing persons whose life is habitually characterized by sins and evil works, both in public and private. This could refer to the public festivals connected to worship of false gods. We often listen to others of all age groups say, 'I am going out to rave; and have a good time, because I only live once'. Many have lost their lives over raving; some attend all night parties and never live to return to their homes. This happens more frequently among younger people who believe that life should be lived in the fast lane; they cut it short without thinking where they will spend eternity.

Let's be careful how we spend our time, time is precious, and irreversible. The Christian believer should have no lot, or part in this destructive behavior of reveling.

Dear God, as we lift our hearts to You, we ask You in the name of Jesus Christ to grant awareness of wrong living. Father, help us to put on the whole amour that we will withstand the wiles of the devil. When we are tempted to do wrong, remind us of who we are in You, Lord Jesus. Thank You in Jesus Christ's precious name. Amen.

The sins we have looked at may be divided into four groups to show the severity of them: Impurity: this is Adultery, Fornication, Uncleanness and Lasciviousness.

In the powerful name of Jesus Christ, I take a command over these destructive sins of the flesh and root out and destroy all these fleshy behaviors; they will not dominate the lives of God's people.

Sins that are connected with pagan worship and religions include idolatry and witchcraft. Idolatry has to do with the worship of false gods. Witchcraft has to do with manipulation and rebellion.

In Jesus Christ's name I declare that these sins will not rule the hearts of God's chosen people. We are no more under the curse, we have been made free from the tight hold of Satan and his destructive force, and we are now under grace.

Sins of temper include hatred/variance (disorder), emulations (jealousies), wrath, strife, seditions (division), heresies, envy and murder. These are devilish behaviors and have their root in a loveless heart. In the mighty name of Jesus Christ I denounce these practices from operating in the lives of God's people, they shall no longer have a hold, but they are cancelled and erased with the all-powerful blood of Jesus Christ.

Sins that are connected to drunkenness include reveling, excessiveness and such like. These are the deadly works of the flesh that come from a sinful nature following the fall.

The child of God will and can never be able to function while these deadly and unfruitful works of darkness are operating in their lives. They must be erased and cancelled by the blood of Jesus. The sinful nature and attitude will put up a resistance to their exit from our lives but we are not alone, we have the Holy Spirit as our Helper.

The believer may still experience daily problems in pleasing God, but by praying and reading the word they will be an over-comer. As we make our confession that sin shall not and will not have dominion over us, let us remember we are not under the law but under grace. Satan is the master of deception; he knows our weak points, and he exploits them wherever possible in a truly devastating manner. If we make a mistake it usually leads to another, and finally sin no longer lies at the door but has entered in. Too often we fail to realize how little spiritual strength we have, when we need it most. May God help us to remain strong in the Lord and in the power of His might so that our prayers can be effective.

When we are living in the Spirit, praying in the Spirit, walking in the Spirit, then we will not fulfill the lust of the flesh (Galatians 5:16). Christ has provided deliverance from the bondage of sin to make it possible to live victoriously. The Holy Spirit cannot abide in us if our worldly passions and desires have not been crucified with Christ.

No one is without sin, but as soon as we confess our sins and repent, God forgives, even though sinful thoughts and actions do creep back into our lives. We all need ongoing cleansing, moment by moment. Thank God He provides forgiveness by His mercy when we ask Him for it. We should make confession and repent regularly. The first step toward a Christian life is utter dissatisfaction with sin and unrighteousness that leads to true repentance, and ultimately results in salvation.

It is of vital importance to ask God to apply the blood of Jesus to our hearts on a regular basis so that these deadly sins may not take root in our hearts. Only then can we have confidence that God hears us when we pray.

Join me in prayer.

Father, I thank You and praise Your great name that You are able to keep Your children from all these destructive behaviors.

Father, You have not given us the spirit of fear, but of love and a sound mind. Help us to be aware that our bodies are Your temple, therefore we ask You for continual cleansing in the blood of Jesus Christ, Your Son.

I ask You in the name of Jesus Christ that Your people may put on the whole armor that they may be able to withstand the wiles of the devil. Help us, O Lord, to realize that You have given to us power over all the works of the flesh.

Father God, we cry out to You for Your strength to stay strong, for Your patience, and Your understanding to stay focused, ever abiding in Your word to be an over-comer. We humbly ask these mercies in Jesus Christ's name.

Amen

12

Fruit Of The Spirit

The fruit of the Spirit is the spontaneous work of the Holy Spirit in us. The fruit refers to a set of character traits that the Spirit produces and which are found in the nature of Christ. They are the by-products of Christ's control; we can't obtain them by trying to get them ourselves, in our own strength or wisdom. If we want the fruit of the Spirit to grow in us, we must join our lives to His life (John 15: 4,5). We must know Him, love Him, remember Him, and imitate Him. As a result, we will fulfill the intended purpose of the law to love God and our neighbor. If we have a longing to be filled with the Spirit, He will grant our request.

There are nine parts to the fruit, representing just one fruit, and they each complement one other. The Holy Spirit directs the working and flow so they are in harmony and cannot function without each other. They are like a fruit that has several segments, having the same taste and functioning.

Here are the nine graces that we must possess in order to function and live a victorious Christian life: Love, Joy, Peace, Long-suffering, Gentleness, Goodness, Faith, Meekness, and Temperance.

Which of these qualities would you desire the Spirit to produce in you? Let us try and define each segment of the fruit.

Love

What is love?

LOVE is a force as strong as death, it cannot be killed by time or disaster, and it cannot be brought by any price, because it is freely given. Love is priceless and even the richest king could not buy it. Love must be accepted as a gift from God and shared within the guidelines that God provides. Married couples should accept the love of their spouse as God's gift and strive to make their love a reflection of the perfect love that comes from God Himself.

Love is the willing sacrificial giving of oneself for the benefit of another without thought of anything in return. God's love is love in its purest and holiest manifestation, and is called Agape love. It is the love that God sends and keeps sending. He sends it on the deserving and the undeserving, on the responsive and on the unresponsive. While we were still sinners God loved us and sent us a love message wrapped in infant flesh. Love is the glue that holds all other graces in place, When we truly love someone we will take an interest in their safety and happiness, and will care what happens to them.

So then, we can understand that love can be a wide subject, but it also can be a small subject if we do not allow our love to have its free course in a right manner.

I could not begin to write about God's love. It would take an ocean of ink to write about the love of God. The love of God is God's gift to mankind (see John 3:16). The songwriter truly penned well, that to write about the love of God would drain the ocean dry, it is so vast, rich and sweet. However, let us look at a few statements on this four-letter word as described in Corinthians 13, which is often called the Love Chapter.

- **AFFECTIONATE LOVE:** to be kindly affectionate one to another, with brotherly love. This statement signifies not only to love but also to be in a readiness and inclination to give love.

- **RESPONSIVE LOVE:** to honor and prefer one another. We should be ready to take notice of the gift and graces and performances of our brethren, and value them accordingly. We should be more pleased to hear applauses for others rather than for ourselves.

- **LIBERAL LOVE:** to make distribution to the necessities of the saints. It would be 'mock love' to show only a verbal expression of kindness while we see our brethren struggling or going without.

- **SYMPATHETIC LOVE:** to rejoice with those who rejoice, and weep with those who weep. When we possess true love we will also feel the sorrows and groans of others as though they were our own. Sympathizing love does not envy those that are prospering, but rejoices for their success.

- **UNITED LOVE:** when we are of the same mind toward others. We will agree in affection, endeavoring to be all one, wishing the same good to others and sharing in their interests.

- **CONDESCENDING LOVE:** not to mind high things, but condescend to men of low estate. It is impossible to have true love without lowliness. In order to love one another right we must be willing to stoop to the menial of office duties in kindness and for the good of others. Therefore, love becomes a condescending grace.

- **A LOVE THAT ENGAGES US** is as much as lies in

- us. We should live peacefully with all men, even those who are difficult – we must try. If we seek God's help He will increase our love even to the unlovable.

- **These are some of the meanings of love:**

- **AGAPE LOVE** describes God's love. It indicates a choice to serve God, to love our neighbor as ourselves, to love without expecting something in return. God decided to love us while we were yet sinners, because that is His nature, to love, because God is love (1 John 4:8).

- **EROS:** describes self-centered love, as in having sexual desire and physical attraction. It describes romantic love.

- **STORGE:** alludes to affectionate love, especially among members. This does not appear in the New Testament. Paul uses it to command us to be 'kindly affectionate to one another' (Romans 12:10).

- **PHILIA:** refers to high esteem and affection, the reflection in the loving concern that friends have for one another. This is also the love that a woman has for her children. This word is from the city of Philadelphia, the city of brotherly love. It is named in Revelation 3, which speaks of warmhearted, spontaneous affection, liking, attractive appeal, and friendship. God never intended for us to have this kind of love for everyone.

The Virtue Of Joy

JOY is gladness of heart, complete happiness as a result of absolute co-ordination of feelings and special perception. Paul discovered the joy of being identified with Christ. Joy belongs to us by the bucketful. The prophet states 'Therefore with joy shall we draw water out of the well of salvation' (Isaiah 12:3).

The joy of the Lord is our strength. The joy of the Lord is not dependent on physical circumstances. It transcends all the trials and frustrations surrounding us, because the source of our joy is Christ Jesus. He alone deserves our adoration, He is worthy of our praise. The psalmist said he would meditate on God's precepts, and whoever does, finds delight in it. Without the joy of the Lord we could not be strong and victorious.

We are encouraged to draw our daily requirement from the fountain from above, the rich source that our Father so lovingly supplies in abundance. Having our heart filled with joy we can sow into the lives of others. It is quite possible for our joy to overflow into the lives of those around us.

Peace

PEACE is tranquility of mind, freeing one from worry and fear. True peace is not established until there is harmony between a man and his Creator. Just before Jesus returned to His Father He said, 'Peace I leave with you... my peace I give unto you... not as the world gives you. Let not your heart be troubled' (John 14:27).

Peace can be maintained through prayer. All our needs must be brought to God in prayer. If problems continue to destroy our inner peace, we should examine our motives to see if all is on the altar of confession so that we can identify what is hindering the peace that we should enjoy. We can also enjoy peace through thinking on whatever things are lovely, clean and pure, and of good report. God will not provide us with peace if we ignore His command to be anxious.

By living a life of obedience we will open the door to enjoying peace. By walking in the Spirit on a daily basis we will experience inner peace. Living a life of peace and satisfaction is beneficial to the mental conditioning necessary for longevity and a productive life. Those who find no peace will fall into despair, and even have a desire to end their own lives. The work of sin is to destroy the body, but righteousness will build up. Righteousness exalts a nation but sin is a reproach to man. We can seek the peace of God that surpasses all understanding; it is a lasting peace, the peace that Jesus Christ left on earth when He ascended to the heavens.

Longsuffering

LONGSUFFERING is to be patient with others; it is the opposite of a short temper. It is a disposition that quietly bears injury. Patience, tolerance and endurance are all part of the refining process as Job explains when he says, 'But he knows the way he takes, when he shall try him I will come forth like pure gold' (Job 23:10). The Book of Hebrews 12: 1-2 states that longsuffering is also the ability to suffer long, to endure suffering without complaining.

Longsuffering is also having the ability to endure pain, hardship and misunderstanding well beyond the normal limit of breaking point. Moses declared that 'The Lord is longsuffering, and of great mercy, forgiving' (see Numbers 14:16). Therefore longsuffering is also the ability to endure suffering without complaining or becoming impatient.

Gentleness

GENTLENESS is kindness, or being kind, considerate, fair and understanding toward fellowmen. True wisdom and knowledge are demonstrated through meekness. Gentleness is like the gentle touch of a mother to a child, and a gentle touch from a nurse to a patient in her care. Gentleness enables us to act fairly with everyone, it encourages harmony among believers. It is often overlooked as a personal trait in our society. Power and assertiveness will gain more respect, even though no one likes to be bullied. Gentleness is love in action, being considerate, meeting the needs of others, allowing time for the other person to talk, and being willing to learn. It is an essential trait for us all to maintain a gentle attitude in relationship with others (1 Thessalonians 2:7). Selfishness cannot demonstrate its actions when gentleness pervades. Gentleness is the opposite of roughness.

Goodness

GOODNESS is generosity, or being kind to everyone. Goodness and righteousness are tied together in such a way that they complement one another and reproduce one another: this gives the two a relative meaning. The steps of a good man are ordered by the Lord, says Psalm 37:33. The good man will declare his position like Joshua who declared, 'as for me and my house, we will serve the Lord' (Joshua 24:15).

'Surely, goodness and mercy shall follow me all the days of my life', says the psalmist.

The Lord is good and His mercy endures forever. Goodness and mercy will follow the believer all the days of his life and he will dwell in the house of the Lord forever.

Faith

FAITH is dependability, to trust in the pledge of another, especially putting hope in Jesus Christ. Faith is also a settled conviction that God will finish the good work which He has begun in us and bring full redemption to the world that struggles under the curse of sin. The attitude of trust and confidence that the Bible calls belief or faith, according to Hebrews 11, is not something we can obtain without help. Faith is a gift from God (Ephesians 2:8). No matter how much faith we have, we can never reach the point of being self-sufficient. Faith is not stored away like money in the bank but growing faith is a constant process of daily renewing our trust in Jesus.

Listen to the words of Jesus as He describes faith, that it is sure, and certain. These two qualities need a secure beginning in God's character; that God is who He says He is. The end point is to believe in God's promises that He will do what He says He will do. God will fulfill His promises even though we may not see the result immediately, yet we should demonstrate true faith in Him. God called the universe into existence out of nothing, He declared that it was to be, and it was. His words have awesome power.

Faith is also an essential element in the virtues of prayer. We must offer up our prayer in faith believing. Faith is an attribute that we should exercise every day. We cannot be saved by deeds of service or without faith in Christ.

Some Assurance about Faith:

Hebrews 11

Someone has said that the gift of faith is seen when faith is carried to its extreme. It is faith that impregnates godly desires with divine power whether they be in spoken words or in acts of obedience.

- ◆ THE WORD OF FAITH is near to you, even in your mouth and in your heart. If we confess with our mouth and believe in our heart that God raised Jesus from the dead we will be saved (Romans 10:9-9); that is the word of faith.

- ◆ THE WORK OF FAITH – Paul reminded the saints not to cease the work of faith, the labor of love, and to remain in the patience of hope in our Lord Jesus Christ (1 Thessalonians 1:3).

- ◆ THE WALK OF FAITH – Paul instructed the saints that they should walk by faith and not by sight.

- ◆ THE DOOR OF FAITH: 'when they were come and had gathered the church together, they rehearsed what God had done with them, and how He had opened the door of faith unto the Gentiles', says Acts 14:27.

- ◆ THE PRAYER OF FAITH will save the sick, and the Lord will raise him up. If there is any that has committed a sin, their sins will be forgiven (James 5:17).

- THE BREASTPLATE OF FAITH: Let us that are of the day being sober putting on the breastplate of faith, and love and as a helmet of salvation through our Lord Jesus Christ (1 Thessalonians 5:8).

- THE SHEILD OF FAITH should be worn so that we can quench all the fiery darts of the wicked one (Ephesians 5:18).

The Characteristic of Meekness

MEEKNESS is gentleness that is courtesy and conservation in one's relationship with others. It is a gentle and quiet spirit within a person. It is inconsistent with, or opposite to, strength. Instead, it is a willingness to submit to even injury for the good of someone else or the good of the kingdom. Matthew 5 states that the meek shall inherit the earth. Meekness is often misunderstood as mere weakness. The person that is meek in character need not concern himself because he knows that he possesses inner strength implanted by the long-term ministry of the Holy Ghost (Numbers 12: 3).

Temperance

TEMPTERANCE is self-control, the ability to harness and control one's passion and lust. Peter gives a worthy challenge: 'And beside this... add to your faith virtue; and to your virtue knowledge; and to knowledge temperance' (2 Peter 1; 5, 6).

Temperance is the final designation in the list of the fruit of the Spirit. This fruit gives spiritual balance to Christian living by which God can be honored and our fellowmen blessed. Our lives are to be an example of temperance, both in physical and spiritual matters. We can demonstrate temperance in our moods, our emotions, responses, and our physical activities. We are admonished in Philippians 5:6 to be anxious for nothing: but in everything by prayer and supplication with thanksgiving let our requests be known unto God. Anxiety will destroy the peace of God.

The peace of God is an abundant measure that will keep our hearts and minds in times when we are tempted to become impatient and anxious... Our minds should be filled with things that are just, pure, lovely, of good report, and worthy of praise. When we feed on these healthy and beneficial thoughts, our minds will have no time to get anxious, but we will seek to discover the next blessing that comes our way. We will want to put out our fleece like Gideon; he did so to find out if the Lord was with him.

The Fruit Of The Spirit In A Poem

Love is the .... Source of Obedience Joy is

the .... Flowers of Holiness Peace is the

Outcome of Trustfulness Long-suffering

is the Partner of Patience Gentleness is the

Daughter of Love **G**oodness is the

Activity of Grace **F**aith is the

Faithfulness of Courage **M**eekness is the

Trait of Christ **T**emperance is the .... Mastery
of Faith.

*To experience an extraordinary flavor put all thesetogether and
serve to others.*

Join me in prayer.

*Father, I come to You in the name of Jesus Christ Your only Son. Father, I
thank you for salvation, the gift of life. Lord my God, I give You praise and
thank You for Your goodness and mercy that follows me everyday.*

*I thank you for the blood of Jesus that was shed on Calvary. You have
said in Your word that if I confess and forsake my sins You are willing to
forgive and to cleanse me from all unrighteousness. I receive cleansing in
Jesus' name.*

*Father, I think of Your greatness in the works of Your hands. You have
fashioned the earth and all that is in it. O God, how great is Your power and
Your might, and the marvelous work of Your hands.*

*I ask You in the name of Jesus Christ to open the eyes of young men in
our nations that they may behold how great and merciful You are. Father,*

grant them a desire for Your word where they will find 'You' as they search the scriptures. They will come to know You as savior of their soul. O Lord, I give You praise from a grateful heart.

Thank You Holy Father, for the transformation You have provided for my redemption. I can say life is better now since You have redeemed me from a life of sin and shame. I give You glory and honor. I ask these mercies in Jesus Christ's name.

Amen

13

Practical Application

Practical application means to put what you know to work. It is like applying all the elements to accomplish effectiveness in prayer. When we include confession, praise and worship, and thanksgiving in our prayers to God, it will produce an unforgettable experience in our prayer life. It will create an atmosphere that will lead us into the presence of the Lord. God's greatness is so overwhelming, so unfathomable, and so indescribable that millions of people are praising Him for who He is. They are bowing down every day before Him in worship for His mercies that endure forever.

It is imperative that when we pray we include all these elements in our prayer. It will make our prayer more effective with positive results. Prayer time will become a time of real satisfaction and fulfillment. We must understand that prayer is the first, second, and third element of the Christian life. We should begin our day with prayer: it should precede and conclude each day. The first act of the soul in the morning should be to draw at the heavenly fountain. We will discover that it will sweeten the taste for that day. Spending a few moments with God at that calm and tranquil fountain is worth more than riches or gold. *Try it. You will never be the same.* The Spirit of God is longing to overflow within us and out to others.

In biblical times men and women made prayer an important part of their lives. They were not afraid to express themselves in tears; bowing down, praying to God who knows them best... Prayer can also be effective in this age of technological development. There is an urgent need for commitment and the Spirit is awaking us to

A Guide to Effective Prayer

pray for our nations. We hear of business development of all sorts, so wouldn't it be a good idea to have an industry of prayer where people can come and learn the importance of prayer?

The sign on the outside of that place could be marked in **BOLD** writing: '***Come and learn the art of Effective Praying!***'

God demands from the individual a total surrender to His for our lives. We may ask how we can develop this irresistible practice of effective prayer. It is by faith in Jesus Christ. It is to make an entrance into one's closet and to close the door behind us; because we will be occupied with the Father for unlimited time.

We are to come in the presence of our heavenly Father, making confessing, sharing petition, offering praise and receiving strength from

Him. What an exciting opportunity the believer has in experiencing mighty results through prayer, in meeting with the Father. This exercise will motivate us to pray without ceasing, depending on our faith and relationship in Jesus Christ.

Men Who Cried In Prayer

PETER:

Peter cried when he saw the boisterous wind. He was afraid and he cried, 'Lord save me.' That cry was nothing like an ordinary cry; it is a cry for help to the One who has power over boisterous winds and waves. When we are in the company of Jesus our Lord, it releases our confidence knowing that He is the master of every situation.

Immediately Jesus stretched forth His hand and caught him and said to him, 'O ye of little faith, why did you doubt?' When Jesus is near we will not come to any harm, all we have to do is call out to Him. He will come to our rescue (Matthew 14:30).

DAVID:

David cried, 'Lord search me!' The cry of David reflects his dependency upon God. He was confident that God would save him from his enemies. He said, 'The Lord shall save me...he shall hear my voice.' David was not merely seeking answers, although it was an expected result of his prayer. But in the midst of oppression he sought deliverance and was confident that God would save and deliver him from his enemies. David said, 'As for me, I will call upon the Lord, and the Lord will save me. Evening and morning and at noon, will I pray, and cry aloud, and He shall hear my voice' (Psalm 55:16-17 and Psalm 139:33).

SAMSON:

Samson cried, according to Judges 16: 28-30, when he found himself in the territory of his enemies. He cried, 'Lord remember and strengthen me.' In spite of Samson's past God still answered his prayer and destroyed the pagan temple and worshippers. God still loved him. He was willing to hear Samson's prayer of confession and repentance and use him one last time. One of the effects of sin in our lives is to keep us from praying. But perfect moral behavior is not a condition for prayer. If God could still work in Samson's situation, He can certainly make something worthwhile out of yours.

We should never allow guilty feelings over past sin to keep us from our only means of restoration. No matter how long you have been away from God He is always ready to hear from you and restore you to a right relationship. Every situation can be salvaged if you are willing to turn again to Him.

HEZEKIAH:

We have read of Hezekiah's attitude to prayer when he received a threatening letter from one of the messengers of Rabshakeh. He read the contents of the letter, and he was very disturbed, so he went into the house of the Lord with the letter. He spread the letter before the Lord so that the Lord might read it, although God already knew the contents of the letter. Hezekiah and his companion Isaiah agreed to pray together on this occasion. It is comforting to have a prayer partner in agreement in times of trouble.

This is a great example to the believer when we are faced with impossible situations from which there appear to be no deliverance. We are not to cast away our confidence which have great recompense. We must believe that God still hears and answers prayer; this will improve our confidence and hope in God's promises.

Hezekiah cried, 'Lord bow down thy ears and hear, open Lord thy eyes and see.' God answered the prayer of Hezekiah in such a mind-blowing manner. God gave the answer to prayer because He has control over men and devils. He had them in His Sovereign grip, they are not free to roam God's planet as they please. God can deal with all of life's difficulties; nothing or no one can shake His domain. He will stand with us… (2 Chronicles 14:16).

The devil is like a roaring lion but we are not ignorant of his devices. Greater is He that is in us than he that is in the world. The devil likes to engage in psychological warfare. In every possible situation he likes to attack our minds, to threaten, to undermine our confidence in God. He inculcates fear and doubt and magnifies and exaggerates our weaknesses. We can understand the reasons why he is called 'a roaring lion' (1 Peter 5:8).

The devil attempts to force us to surrender without argument. His attacks are not always physical darts, but he attacks our mind, and our thoughts. We must learn and train others how to use the shield of faith in order to quench these fiery darts of the enemy through the power of prayer.

We can ask ourselves this question: What would be our response in receiving such a letter from a person displaying such boasting and threatening behavior?

We too have a cry...of help... 'Lord... forgive and strengthen us.'

To revive our prayer life, try these:

+ **PRAYER** must be directed to God. We can take our example from Matthew chapter 6:9.

+ **PRAYER** *must be* made in the name of our Lord Jesus Christ according to Word of God. The Son of God said that if we shall ask anything in His name He will do it (John 14:13).

+ **PRAYER** *must be in faith*: Matthew 21:22 says whatever you shall ask in prayer, it is necessary to believe and to receive.

+ **PRAYER** *must be* linked with avoidance of all known sins. Psalm 66:16 says, 'If I regard iniquity *in my heart the Lord will not hear me.'*

+ **PRAYER** *must be made* without ceasing. In Acts

12:5 Peter was kept in prison, but prayer was made *without ceasing unto God by the church for him.* Prayer must become a life-style.

Bible Warriors who prayed effectively:

STEPHEN prayed before his death. He knelt down and cried with a loud voice and said 'Lord, do not charge them with this sin, and then he fell asleep.' (Acts 7:60)

PETER stood up in the midst of the disciples as they prayed together in the upper room and said, 'Men of Judea and all who dwell in Jerusalem, let it be known to you and heed to my words.' (Acts 2:14) There was a sweet spirit of togetherness when they continued with one accord.

THE APOSTLES prayed for boldness to be lead in the Lord's work. They prayed with one accord and said, 'Lord, you are God who made the heaven and earth and the sea, and all that is in them, who by the mouth of your servant David have said 'Why did the heathen rage, and the people plot vain things'. The kings of the earth took their stand, and the rulers were gathered together against Christ.' When they had finished, the place where they were was shaken, and they were all filled with the Holy Ghost and spoke with boldness.

THE CHURCH prayed when Peter was kept in prison. As the believers were still praying, they heard a knock at the door, it was Peter. He was released from prison by an angel. When Peter and the angel came to the big gate to the entrance of the city, the gate was open on its own accord. The big gates of impossibilities, persecution and trouble swung open and he was brought out safely. God has a way of breaking locks without having to use any means of man-made instruments. *Isn't our God wonderful?* (Acts 25:16)

PAUL says that he does not cease to give thanks for the brethren, making mention of them in his prayers (Ephesians 1:16). He also says, 'I can do all things through Christ which strengthens me' (Philippians 4:13).

Paul's prayer was that God would continue to work in them, especially in three important areas, in *wisdom, revelation,* and *knowledge.* Wisdom speaks of the ability to be skillful in living; revelation expresses the need to learn special lessons and insights that only God can give; and knowledge indicates information and teaching that is centered on God.

MARY said, 'My soul magnifies the Lord and my spirit rejoices in God my Savior, for He has regarded the lowly state of His hand servant. For behold, henceforth all generations shall call me blessed.'

After the death and resurrection of our Lord, Mary played a significant role by going to the tomb early in the morning. This is an indication of the way that love can conquer timidity and fear. There was gloom in Mary's heart when she found that the tomb was empty. Her natural reaction was that some one might have taken her Lord away. She panicked and came to a quick conclusion without entering the tomb with the other women. She said, 'They have taken away the Lord out of the sepulcher.'

Although she thought someone had stolen her Lord, yet she also thought that maybe He did not really die. She had a kind of personal faith and devotion to Jesus that is true love even when she was not sure what really happened to the body of Jesus.

We may want to ask why Mary allowed the other women to look in the tomb while she stayed outside weeping. We can believe that it was her love for Christ that made her act that way. We too can identify with losing a loved one, how sadness and sorrow sometimes blinds our eyes with tears.

However, we must never allow our tears to blind us from the glory of heaven and eternal life. When Mary looked through her tears and peeped into the tomb, she failed to see what Peter and John had seen.

It is so amazing how God gave Mary a vision of two angels sitting where the body of Jesus had been. In her confusion and anxiety, wondering where the body of her Lord was, God stepped in to calm her troubled heart... The angel spoke to her and she gave a reply, but the significance of the message failed to reach her heart. When she turned she saw Jesus standing, she did not know who He was, not until Jesus called her by her name. When He called her by name it brought back memories to her. All the revelation was in that one word: Mary.

Can you hear His voice calling you to a higher life of praise? He still calls us by our name, He knows our name (Luke 1:46).

JEHOSHAPHAT feared and prayed to the Lord when he received a threatening message from his enemies, that three nations were coming to attack him. In response, he went into the house of the Lord and spread the letter before the Lord. Then he stood up and prayed and said, 'O Lord God of our fathers or you are not the God who is heaven. You rule over the kingdom of this nation. Power and might are in your hand, and no-one can withstand you. O our God, did you not drive out the inhabitants of this land before your people Israel and gave it to the descendants of Abraham your friend?' (Chronicles 20:610)

Jehoshaphat's prayer had several essential ingredients:

- He committed the situation to God, knowing that it is only God who could save the nation.

- He sought God's favor because his people were God's people.

- He acknowledges God's sovereignty over the current situation.

- He praised God's glory, and took comfort in His promises.

- He professed complete dependence upon God, and not himself, for deliverance.

We Need Prayer Champions like:

DANIEL did not shrink when the angry king ordered his death. He found himself in a 'close to death' spot. Daniel had some good praying friends who trusted in their God like he did. Daniel and his friends arranged a prayer meeting, and called on the all-powerful name of God about the problems that they were currently facing. It is so heart warming to have friends to agree in prayer, when there is a crisis. When you are in a state of panic, it will confirm your hopelessness, but prayer will confirm your hope in

A Guide to Effective Prayer

God. Daniel and his friends trusted in God to deliver them, and it was a success (Daniel 2:17).

DAVID said, 'At night I rise up to give thanks for His righteous laws. I am a friend of those who fear God to all who follow His precepts' (Psalms 119:63).

PAUL was not afraid to be killed by the haters of the gospel for the sake of the gospel. (Acts 19: 29-30).

JOHN, who on the Isles of Patmos because of the word of God and his testimony, during a time when the Christian church was facing severe persecution, stood the test and recorded what he saw and heard. He left us a true record of the things that were and what was to come *(Revelation 1:9).*

NEHEMIAH, another praying champion, heard that the wall of Jerusalem had not been repaired but remained broken down. He wept yet prayed and anticipated the improving of the situation that he was facing. Nehemiah started out with prayer because it is the way... Heartfelt prayers like Nehemiah's can help to clarify any situation. By the time Nehemiah finished his prayer he knew what action he was supposed to take. He put all his resources, his knowledge, experience and organizational skills together to remedy the problem (Nehemiah 1: 4).

It is encouraging to know that when we pray in difficult situations God will intervene, everything will fall into proper perspective. I feel confident that I belong to God who knows all about me, I can trust Him with my everything. He knows where I live, and what I am thinking, and He knows my heart and desires. In today's closing hour, 'Oh that we too would find our place and apply these prayer elements when we pray and seek God's mercy on behalf of ourselves and others.' It gives a warm feeling of belonging when we pray with assurance and include all elements in our prayer. God will be pleased, and our prayer will be felt even by ourselves. Men are advised to pray and not to faint. Living a life of faith and prayer will help us to become joint-heirs with our Father.

Prayer should be like the air that we breathe, without it we are unable to live. We pray, we praise our God, we adore Him, we give Him thanks; we send up prayers for others, we pray for ourselves and also our enemies, and the list goes on. There must not be a void in our lives when we have nothing to do. No, it should never be said that we are bored. Let us be reminded to turn to prayer wherever and whenever we need help from Almighty God, He's just a breath away.

Join me in prayer.

Holy Father, I come to You in the name of Jesus Christ Your Son. I just want to bless Your Holy name. Thank You for Your great salvation. Thank You for Your peace that surpasses my understanding. Father, Your loving kindness is better than life. Oh, how much I praise You for being so thoughtful about Your creation.

O Father, I ask You to tabernacle with us, as we seek to dwell in the secret place where we can feel the warmth of Your presence. Lord, we long to rise in the arms of faith and be closer drawn to You. Father, we want to have an intimate relationship with You as Savior and Lord.

Father, please remember our families, ministers of the gospel, our brothers and sisters, young people, the old, the poor, and the disabled in our communities, children who have lost their parents, governments, teachers, doctors, nurses, patients; Lord, please remember us all. Let Your mercies and Your goodness ever surround us, so that we will always be mindful of You, we ask this in the loving name of Jesus Christ.

Amen

14

Prayer And The Church

The strength of a building is only as good as the foundation. The foundation of the Christian is in Christ Jesus. The 'Rock' on which God builds His church has been identified as Jesus Christ in His work of salvation by dying on the cross. It is said that Peter was the first leader in the church of Jerusalem. The confession of faith that he made is what all subsequent believers would give. It seems most likely that the rock would refer to Peter as the leader, for his function, but not necessarily his character. Just as Peter had revealed the true identity of Christ, so Jesus revealed Peter's true role. Peter reminds Christians that we are the church that is built on the foundation and the apostles and prophets, with Jesus Christ as the cornerstone (1 Peter 2:4). All believers are joined to the church by faith in Jesus Christ as Savior.

The Church of Christ also includes officers, teachers, preachers, parents and others that are born again into the family of God. It is expected that the members of the church will develop a high quality standard, having the right doctrine and right living to meet God's standard. It is important that each church member becomes matured spiritually, sensitive and doctrinally sound. If we are to fit into the church, the body of Christ, we must live a life that is acceptable before God. We must endeavor to fit into the pattern that is provided by Christ.

It is imperative that we keep the fire of prayer alive in our churches so that believers can join together in unity with enthusiasm and burning with holy joy. For by grace we are saved and not by ourselves, it is a gift from God.

We are not saved by any merit of our own; it is because of the grace of Jesus Christ. Our responsibility is to receive it in faith, because God does not impose salvation on any one, but each person is encouraged to accept this gift in faith.

Therefore a prayer program should have a place in the church, as well as the Sunday school. The Sunday school is the place where the young people can be trained to become good citizens and followers of Christ and to make a difference. The Sunday school can be the place for setting a solid foundation. Children should be taught from an early age and be taught at home by parents to say even simple prayers until they are able to pray for themselves. We are admonished by the word of God that parents should 'train up a child in the way he should go' so that when he is old he will not depart from it.

It is necessary for a loving parent to discipline a child, which should be done in love. The greatest responsibility that God gives to a parent is to nurture and guide their children. A lack of discipline will put parent's love in question; it shows a lack of concern for the character development of their children. Without discipline children would be heading for long-term disaster. Without correction, children will grow up with no fear of God, or the understanding of doing right, or wrong, and without any direction in their lives. To discipline our children is an act of love, although our efforts may not make our children wise, but it will encourage them to seek the wisdom that only comes from God.

There is absolutely nothing that could prevent God from loving us the way that He does and nothing that we could ever do to allow Him to love us less, not our character flaws, our failures or our regrets. How great is the love that the Father lavishes upon us. *It is His unconditional love…*

Children and young people should be reminded how God loves them. He loves them so much that He gave His only begotten Son to die for them, even when they were not yet born. We are to tell them that God will stretch out the 'rainbow of hope to them for the asking, seeking, and to those who knock'. The greatest thing one person can do for another is to light them a '*candle of hope that they may see the goodness of the Lord and in turn accept Him as Lord and Savior of their lives*'.

People who attend church are from all walks of life; they are of different ages, color, and backgrounds who rub shoulders with each other, who maybe facing despair, disappointment, anxiety. They come to church seeking hope that a word, or a prayer of faith may come from the person who is leading. In this instance we have to be careful how we live our lives outside of church. We will never know who these people are that attend church. Therefore, we must be a light shining very bright as we live our Christian life outside of church.

Our light must shine at home, in communities, places of work and leisure, outside of where we worship. People need to follow footprints that lead them in the right direction. We must first be an example where we live, work, study, and in our community; our behavior must match up with our testimony.

There should be a department of prayer in every church, because it is where we draw our spiritual strength. In this room with the engine in full working order we will fill up our tanks for battle in our spiritual, emotional and physical struggles. God's word is another vital source of our strength. The word of faith is another source of strength, it often comes just at the right time; sometimes it comes during the midst of trials, temptation, or a time of suffering.

A prayer that is coupled with the word from the preacher will act as antidote for sick, lame, deaf, dumb and disabled soul. The word fittingly spoken will cut through the heart of the unbeliever so that the Spirit of the Lord can go in and bring conviction.

I know of a church that organizes prayer groups and nominates prayer captains to be leaders. Prayer can be a personal activity; people can pray at different times and for different needs. This is a worthwhile method that brings success on the part of who does the prayer and for whom the prayer is prayed. We can use the method like a chain; prayers that are linked to other groups at every hour of the day or night for a specific person or thing. This method can be heartwarming, soul-stirring. If we should put prayer to the test it will be victorious every time we bow our knees and heart.

The church can be described as casualty where the sick, lame, deaf, and people with incurable infirmities come daily for help. People come for all reasons, some for emotional or spiritual help, and others maybe for physical. Whatever is the case, it can be an excellent opportunity to visit places like these, where people come daily for help. We can take the opportunity to witness, and win the lost for Christ. People are more responsive to receive the good news where there is sickness or problems that they cannot deal with.

The lame man who was laid at the gate Beautiful was in the right place to receive his healing as the apostles came that way to pray. He received more than what he had expected. He received healing of body, soul and spirit. What a package! His healing enabled him to rise up and walk; it was better than the money that he had asked and hoped for. The name of Jesus Christ is powerful to set the stage right for all times and situations. Will you rise up out of that long drawn out situation, and leap for your deliverance? This is the moment; this is the acceptable time of deliverance and victory.

Our duty is to present the gospel in a simple and prayerful manner so that people can understand the meaning of salvation. We must equip ourselves in prayer and the word, depending on the Holy Spirit to minister to each person that has a need. There is help for all at the cross, the ground is level. Christ is our high priest; He bore our sins on the cross. Every stripe that Jesus received was for our healing. It is said that the 39 lashes that was placed on His back represent the 39 kinds of sickness and disease that people may suffer from. So we don't have to bear, or be satisfied with sickness and disease, we can call on Jesus' name as our refuge and strength, and a present help in trouble. He is acquainted with such calls from His children. God is concerned about all areas of humanity, so should the church be...

For example, man's total being, with its various needs, physical, mental, and spiritual, is infested with the wrong attitude to life until the Spirit of the Lord comes in to do a shift. We are prone to wander aimlessly looking for other solutions to our problems. The church is a company of resurrected ones, those who were once dead in sin, and are now alive in Christ. So then the born again believer is acquainted with the cry from the people who come to church for whatever reason.

Ministers of the gospel are in a positive position to offer salvation, prayer, counseling, good advice, support, all together. It is so easy to become attached to a spiritual leader, because of how they treat you. It is natural to feel loving toward the leader, but we must be warned how we should show gratitude to our leaders. Any true leader is a representative of Christ and has nothing to offer that God has not given him. We never allow our loyalty to cause strife, slander, or broken relationships; please make sure that our deepest loyalty is to Christ and not to human agents.

The church is the place where people should run to for help. We should be careful in our approach, how we treat students, employees, church members, children, young people and older people. We should ask ourselves the question: Does this person need guidance, or need to be nurtured? Sometimes we can act a bit heavy-handed on those who may not be in our circle of friends. It is a good idea to remind ourselves that, however holy we may feel, we were in the same position as those people we now have to minister to. Let us allow the grace of God to speak to us at all times, regarding how to treat each other.

Some people will choose to attend church for a burial, dedication of babies, weddings and other occasions, like Christmas and Easter Bank holidays. Other times people wait until they are having a crisis before they decide to attend church, and so they go on. But whatever happens the church should be a place of prayer, and ready to give support.

Christ continues to be the High Priest for the believer today. He has met the eternal requirements that the Father required. He intercedes to the Father just as the High Priest did in the Old Testament. When the church prays, our prayers are not in vain as 'Christ can be touched with the feeling of our infirmities'. To be touched is to suffer with or to share the same pain or experiences.

Christ is the most qualified person to hear and answer our prayers. He listens and He is involved in every prayer that we pray because He has experienced the depth of our heart's cry. Some may think that psychology could take the place of prayer, but it cannot. Others think that having a good education and culture can take the place of prayer, but our present problems show us that none of these man-made regulations are sufficient to take the place of prayer.

The believer's duty is to maintain this program and encourage others to do the same. Paul reminds the believer to come boldly to the throne of grace, that they may obtain mercy, and find grace to help in time of need.

Prayer should be one of the main elements coupled with faith in preaching, giving Bible study in our church. It would seem that preaching has become first place, and teaching followed by classes, such as learning the art of dancing, rather than encouraging people the simple art of praying. The same emphasis that is placed on teaching, preaching, seminars, singing and musical events should be no less when it is time to pray. It is prayer that keeps our spiritual battery fully charged.

The fellowship of the church should be opened to all, because it has been built by God, who is the Father of all. We all can share these words of Paul to the Ephesian believers: He said, 'Blessed be the God and Father of our Lord Jesus Christ, who hath blessed us with all spiritual blessings in heavenly places in Christ' (Ephesians 1:3).

Therefore a prayer-less ministry would become a powerless ministry. Church history proves that the ministry of prayer makes the ministry of the word more powerful. A prayer-less pulpit is one of empty words with no spiritual weight or value, and nothing to minister to the spirits of men.

Read carefully the words by a famous writer and preacher who wrote, 'Once we have the Holy Spirit, our prayers will be implemented by our praying in the spirit. Communication with God in prayer will become easier, because we are using His preferred and most direct method. Our prayers will have superior guidance and understanding, and will no longer have a selfish attitude.

'When we are wrestling with a situation and are nearly thrown down, we can ask the Holy Spirit to nerve the arm to ease the pain as we continue holding until He blesses us.

'Let us consider how the Holy Spirit is the chariot of prayer. Prayer maybe the chariot, the desire may draw it forth, but the Spirit is the very wheel whereby it moves.' (Spurgeon)

It is rightly said that a powerless church is useless and cannot function without prayer. When the church engages all that is necessary to the reaping of souls then we can truly say we are fulfilling the great commission. Jesus said 'that the harvest is truly plenteous, but the laborers are few'.

There seems to be enough professional preachers to turn the world to God, if all of them should be active in gathering the harvest. Many people admire the status of being preachers, but they don't have a compassionate heart for souls. Some take preaching as a career, there are others who see it as a way of earning a living, but preachers should be willing to win the lost for Christ, at any cost. We can agree that some are called to the ministry of soul winning, while others went with their own inner agenda. But whatever the case, we must be true and faithful, because time is coming when every man's work will be tried.

Jesus continues His discourse with His disciples to pray, therefore, that the Lord of the harvest would send forth laborers into the harvest. The solution lies in prayer and faith, believing. We must continue our prayer ministry for workers in the body of Christ. Our Father is the Lord of the harvest, and Christ His Son is employed in the harvest field. It is important that the right kind of workers are released, those who are equipped by the Holy Spirit, and who are consecrated to the needs of people, and not for their own gain. They are those who are instruments of mercy, having a servant's heart.

It will be impossible for the church to meet all the needs of the congregation and the wider society, unless all believers are engaged in a life of prayer. Still one cannot depend on others to carry out this assignment; we must take the responsibility to pray without ceasing for ourselves and for one another.

It is believed that few people ever leave a deeply, spiritual, prayer-ruled church to join the religious cults… because prayer prevails and can satisfy earthly problems in the name of Jesus. We cannot plead that we are too busy to pray, prayer should be our lifestyle and practiced as a daily routine. Prayer is a responsibility that we must fulfill, by doing our best to maintain this important assignment. A church cannot be built spiritually without prayer. A number of people can be drawn through personal work or eloquence, but the building of a real spiritual body is only possible through prayer.

No matter how weak or inadequate a Christian may feel, he can rely on the Holy Spirit to work through him in his efforts to win the lost. Soul saving is at the heart of the church. It is the greatest business in the world. It is like the greatest hour when a surgeon holds a scalpel at the end of which is life or death for the patient. It is as the greatest hour when a lawyer faces a jury with the conviction that if he makes a mistake, an innocent man will be hanging, and a family will be disgraced forever. But the greatest time any human being ever faces is the hour when he stands before a man hastening to his condemnation and a commission to offer him a pardon that is to last for the eternity.

A question is poised here: can there be any question about the help of the Holy Spirit in the great work of witnessing? Let us think about this the next time you and I have the opportunity to talk to someone who we meet about the saving power of our Lord Jesus Christ. Every church should be concerned in evangelism to win souls for the Kingdom. This could be implemented by setting up its members in regular prayer sessions.

The outcome will be virtuous. There would be fewer problems among members, families and communities, the unity of the church will be at peace, and the unsaved will notice the difference in our attitude toward each other. The unsaved will want to make a commitment to accept the Lord and serve Him as their personal Savior when we as believers take time to look in God's big mirror and live holy. We will see ourselves as God sees us. We must be willing to change our attitude and do the right thing. Time is important, let us be careful how we spend each day.

It will be worth our while to take an assessment of how our spiritual life is going. We will discover if we still have that spiritual thirst for prayer and reading God's word. Then we can do the necessary adjustment about the findings. Looking in God's mirror will reveal the truth that will set us free. The pastor and church leaders would have fewer problems with church members, if each of us carry out regular assessments on our own lives. Each member should develop a lively conscience about themselves, and about the things of God. I personally believe that the Church is a wonderful place; it is a good institution to be a part of. *How about you?*

Join me in prayer.

Sovereign Lord, I praise You for Your beautiful creation. Blessed be Your great name. O Lord, You are good and Your mercies endure forever. God, You have stretched out the heavens like a curtain, You have covered Yourself with light as a garment. You appoint the moon to give light on earth; the sun to shine by day, O Lord, how excellent is all the works of Your hand.

Lord, let Your virtue enfold us through the blessed name of Jesus. Father, I bring the ministers of the gospel that You have commissioned to preach, teach and make disciples. Father, in the name of Jesus I ask that You will revive, refresh and anoint them afresh to carry out Your command.

Father, I ask You for a burning desire to pray for the Church and the activities, that we as believers will be more willing to carry out the task that is assigned to us.

Truly the time that we are now living in is increasingly wicked, so Your ministers need more of You than ever. Grant them more understanding and wisdom to deal with people of all races and color. Father, increase their awareness to Your coming that they may preach Your word without fear or favor.

I ask You to visit friends and families across the world and remind them of the grace that is available to them. Let them ever be mindful of Your great salvation which You offered to the 'whosoever will'. I ask this in Jesus Christ's name.

Amen

Prayer Arrows

The weapons of our warfare are not carnal, but powerful through God in the pulling down of strongholds (2 Corinthians 6:7).

According to Isaiah 22:6 arrows were carried in quivers on chariots, or they were hung on the back or at the warrior's left side. This was man's invention for us in wartime but prayer is the Christian's weapon to fight against the enemy of our soul.

Therefore prayer arrows are effective faith-based tools. They carry the Holy Ghost anointing with each mission. They bring conviction, hope and faith to the receiver. It is like sending a message marked 'special delivery'. The arrows will reach an exact area of need that is designated. It is like how God sends His word and it does not return to Him void, but accomplishes what it was sent out to do. It is sharper than a two-edged sword. It is said that one end does the cutting and the other end will perform the healing. It will spur the heart of man and bring conviction. It is like a searchlight that can be turned in any direction.

Prayer arrows will always stay sharpened in the word with faith as its strong backup. The believer's responsibility is to maintain their prayer vigil always and constantly, in and out of season. David's reliance upon God was evident in his words to Goliath, when he said, 'You are coming to me with a sword and spear and a javelin but I am coming to you in the name of Jehovah of armies, the God of the battle lines of Israel who you have taunted. This day God will surrender you into my hand, and this entire congregation will know that God does not fight with swords and spears.' (1 Samuel 17: 45-47).

Thank God that we are effectively provided with this powerful tool of prayer, it is great...

It is fulfilling. Hallelujah!

A prayer arrow can travel like the wind; climb the highest mountain, to reach the needs of people anywhere in the world. It is like a prayer that is prayed in faith to heal the sick, and bring deliverance to hurting people. Psalms 7: 13 says, 'God has prepared His deadly weapons; He makes ready His flaming arrows'. He will always fight for His people in times of trouble.

Jesus sent His word and people were healed, of all diseases. Longstanding conditions can be dug and rooted out with a prayer arrow. You can send an arrow of prayer to some one today, they will feel the lift of the Holy Ghost connection, linking them to the Father in Jesus' mighty, all-powerful name, a name that makes hell tremble, and Satan run in terror. You won't be disappointed, you will be glad that you prayed, when you realize what prayer can do. Yes, prayer can do the impossible through Jesus Christ the King of Glory.

Praying for others, no matter where they live, is a work that must be done. It is hard work, but it is very rewarding. It gives a great satisfaction to hear someone say, 'Thank you for praying for me.' This does not have to be a person who is living next door. A prayer arrow can be sent anywhere in the world. Prayer must be in faith as wings to fly near or far. It reaches safely and brings tremendous joy to the person as if that person were living next door. Prayer arrows have no limit in space or distance, it knows no prejudice, it has no interest in itself, and the only set back is if it is sent in the spirit of unbelief. The sender must believe that God is able to do the impossible, and the recipients must also receive the prayer in faith, that it shall be done. So then it is by faith and not by sight. He who comes to God must believe that God is a rewarder to them that diligently seek Him.

Faith will strengthen prayer, aiding the arrow to individual needs, and help to lift up the falling and down trodden in their conditions. It will carry hope for those who are feeling hopeless, it will carry compassion to those who are grieving, it will give peace to those who are experiencing confusion, so no matter what the situation is, there is a solution in prayer and the word of God.

Within the breast of each living being is something wonderful and more mysterious than a beam. It is an arrow of prayer and supplication that will reach even to the backslider and remind them that God is still waiting to receive them.

The believer is also called to put on the amour of light, to lengthen the prayer cord, widening prayer gaps, strengthening the wheels of prayer, having a vision of prayer to be used effectively. It is also useful to study the life of men who knew how to pray and what happened, how victory was won, a lion's mouth locked without any man involved, fire put out without water, prison doors opened without the use of a key and many more testimonies that are recorded.

Many times we wonder why the test comes at a particular time when we have just got over one hurdle, but if God is leading you, you can expect to have more trouble, more disappointment, more let downs from friends and families. Be prepared, it will be a sign and a token that God is doing something within you. He is digging a well in you, out of which will spring the water of life. Or He is sinking a shaft in you because of the gold that lies so deep that this is the only way to ensure it will get out. If He chooses to use the threshing floor, this is because it is the only way of separating the grain from the straw. If God chooses to lay you out in the dew, it is not until every fiber of wrong that is in you is rooted out that you can produce the fine linen of righteousness. At every single step He is leading you to a nobler manhood; to the very substance of your being; for more strength to endure.

The devil can send out his arrows to harm the Christian, but think of the mighty arrow of prayer in the hands of every believer. Prayer will do devastating damage to the kingdom of darkness. His arrows are the negative states of mind that destroy our happiness; we are possessed with true happiness that comes from God, with a healthy state of mind, which is of God.

Prayer can be compared to a bow, the promise is like the arrow, and faith is like the hand which draws the bow and sends the arrow to the hearts of men and women with messages of salvation. The bow without the arrow is of no use, and the arrow without the bow is of little worth, and both, without the strength of the hand are of no purpose. Neither the promise without prayer, nor prayer without the promise, or faith or both without faith, will avail the Christian anything.

We need each other to make the journey. Cooperation coupled with zeal will accomplish what zeal alone cannot do. It is inspiring and soul satisfying that we include all elements in our prayer to accomplish our spiritual goals (Psalms 44:6-8).

Father, we adore You, we praise You, we thank You, and bless Your holy name, and we are now ready to move forward in our prayers. Father, give us Your guidance to use this prayer arrow effectively, to cut, pull down, and root out, and take authority over the works of Satan in the all powerful name of Jesus Christ. Amen.

Prayer Nuggets

- Give prayer a large place in your church programs.

- Do not only teach prayer but practice the art of prayer.

- Pray in your home, inviting all family members to join when possible.

- Create an interest on the prayers of biblical people.

- Search for passages of the Bible that relate to victorious praying.

- Plan a prayer service with retired adults, then with the young people.

- Sing prayer songs, make melody in your heart, remind your friends to pray.

- Replace text messages with prayer messages to your friends.

- Hand out information on how effective prayer can be to individuals.

- Educate each other about prayer and how it can and will prevail.

- Join up with friends for a prayer session, encourage personal time of devotion.

- Write a daily prayer journal, and share it with a close friend.

* Tell some one that you are praying for them, they will feel happy.

* Plan a prayer walk; you can share your faith while walking.

* Put prayer stickers on your fridge in the kitchen, or the bedroom and bathroom.

* Be persistent in prayer, it will build your faith and allow you to trust God.

* Express gratitude for every answered prayer. Pray with faith and expectancy.

* Prayer will show your sins, so that you will repent.

* Prayer will help us to develop wisdom, and treat others fairly.

* Prayer will touch our hearts and our pockets to give to worthy causes.

* Prayer will help us to forgive others, and be happy when they prosper.

Join me in prayer.

Our Gracious God and Heavenly Father, we adore Your great name that is above other names.

Be exalted, O Lord, in Your strength as we sing praises to Your name. You alone are worthy to receive glory and honor. Father, You are my rock and fortress therefore my heart trusts in You. Lord, our hearts long for You; we yearn for the fellowship of the Holy Spirit the Comforter.

Father, may we ever maintain the desire to keep searching Your word, so that we may apply our hearts to the truth that will set us free.

Father, be pleased to grant understanding of Your word that I may know how to apply it to my heart. I pray for Your anointing on my life and on the lives of my readers.

Father, as Your word declares, Your word is Spirit and life, so grant us the true meaning of new life in Jesus' name.

Father, I ask You to bless every person that holds a copy of this book in their hand. Help them to feel blessed, that each word that has been written may be a channel of blessing to themselves, their families, their friends, and all who will share in the reading.

Father, I pray that You will widen our capability to grasp the truth of Your word and to put them into practice.

I ask this in Jesus Christ's name.

Amen

15

Our Motives In Prayer

Jesus taught His disciples that when they pray, they should not do as the hypocrites, for they do this to be seen of men, and as a result they have their reward. God reads the hearts of everyone. Our lives and hearts are like open books to Him. He knows if we are sincere or merely putting on a show so let's not waste precious time. Let us ask the Holy Spirit to help us pray effectively. The avenues of prayer are so vast that we need not keep prayer as a small employment, we can launch out into the deep and get ourselves ready for a mighty draft. We are urged to develop right motives in our prayer life, with no hidden agenda.

There are various ways and types of prayer. We can pray quietly, reverently in praise and worship, praying in warfare, or singing in the spirit, praying in tongues (although I have never personally experienced this gift, but I have listened to others who have the gift of tongues) and many more. Perhaps you can add to the list with your experience.

We should pray out of a sincere heart, like when Hannah went to the temple and sent up her prayer in deep sorrow of heart because she wanted a son. The priest saw her pouring out her sorrow to God, and he was mistaken and thought she was drunk. She explained to him that she was not drunk, but she was having sorrow of heart and seeking her God who helps all who seek Him. She said, 'My heart rejoices in the Lord, my horn is exalted in the Lord'. She brought passion to her prayers. She got to the point out of desperation; she fought with some of the same weapons available in our day. She demonstrated the weapon of prayer, consistency, persistency, praise, passion and faith (1 Samuel 2:1).

The believer has no life or strength, or spiritual power, but all comes from God who continually supplies grace, strength, and ability. We are joined to Christ by faith and are united with Him in a mysterious union through the Holy Spirit. Only through this arrangement can we stand strong in faith, able to run the race that is set before us.

The primary motive of prayer then is sincerity.

Here Jesus tells us that we should not be as the hypocrites when engaged in prayer. These people manifest the same attitude in prayer as they would do in other business. Prayer is a serious virtue and should be treated so. If one should be given the privilege to approach an earthly king in his palace with a request, it would take days of preparation to get ourselves in order.

If one was visiting the Royal Palace, we would dress in our Sunday best and make other preparations, like having our hair done, nails and teeth polished. After all this we might not even be given the opportunity to see the Royals. Maybe one of the king's footmen would be sent to take the message or the request to the king on our behalf. But Christ our heavenly King is so willing and delighted to listen to us in person and does not send anyone else. As a matter of fact, He bids us to 'Come boldly to His throne of grace.' Halleluiah! Won't you accept this invitation and go to Him? And by the way, let us remember what He says about when He returns. He will be coming for us Himself. He won't be sending one of His angels, no, He will come and take us to our heavenly home. We should make it our duty to be ready to go with Him when He comes. Glory to God in the highest! Halleluiah!

We are told that among the Jewish people, prayer was sometimes reduced to a systematic schedule so that the hour of prayer might overtake a man anywhere. It is understood that the hypocrites and the Pharisees might desire to be overtaken especially in public places, where they can display their pretentious piety. Although the synagogues were places of prayer they would prefer to pray in the market places where they could be seen and heard by men. This desire to be seen by men will constitute an evil motive in prayer. It sends out the wrong message instead of a message of hope. They use prayer with a wrong motive.

The Christian is therefore exhorted to seek divine approval, rather than human admiration. It does not matter where we pray, but it is the spirit in which we pray. Man continues to search for God through the medium of prayer. If we want to develop a strong relationship with

God through prayer it will not happen overnight. It takes perseverance and patience to stick it out even when we do not feel like praying.

As one gets closer to God our Father, it is evident that the relationship will be felt and noticed more closely. God is holy and wants His children to be holy also. Therefore it is imperative to check our motives whether we have faith or not. There could be little foxes wandering about so we are warned to examine ourselves. The old Adamic nature of man likes to pull a fast one and creep back with its deadly works of the flesh. We are advised to put on the whole amour of God to withstand the wiles of the devil.

Therefore our motives in prayer should be one of faithfulness, and having a right attitude. We should pray without fail, but develop a right attitude toward God and man. We can find virtue in prayer if we sincerely ask, seek, knock.

We are encouraged to set a time for prayer early in the day, when we are fresh and alert and not waiting until we are tired and exhausted at the end of the day. There are times when the brain cells are locking down and need to rest. It is so easy to get into bed, and say 'I will pray later'. Believe me from experience it will never work. It is wise to pray earlier, we can choose standing up if we are feeling tired. Walk about the room and pray, you will experience that by the time you get into praise and worship you won't realize that you were feeling tired.

There are several lessons to be learned from our Lord. Even when He was tired, weary, sad, and facing the cross, He took the time to pray to His father. That is enough to enhance our appreciation of our Lord. So the next time you feel too tired to pray remember how Jesus prayed throughout His Gethsemane experience.

God has stamped His image on the soul of the believer and He has provided the power to keep it there. He has invested within the very soul of His children the principle of spiritual values; this was not intended that the believer goes on sinning. It is a reminder to the believer that He who has begun a good work is able to perform it until the day of Jesus Christ. It will cost us self-denial to obtain the power of the Spirit. It costs self-surrender, humility and yield to gain most things of God. It will cost the perseverance of long waiting and the faith to trust.

When we seek God's power through effective fervent prayer we can say with assurance that 'nothing will be impossible with God'. Our duty is to make room to receive the gift of the Spirit. It is imperative that the believer lives a life of consistency in prevailing prayer. God expects us to walk in the Spirit. It is very much essential to please God.

Many people pray, but few proportion the fervency, humility, and perseverance in their prayers to the greatest of the blessing for which they pray. When we follow Christ in sunlight and laughter, we must also remember that there will be storms, and darkness. We can trust God in the storms of life, and love Him more as we hold on tighter to His strong arms.

The more we pray, is the more we rejoice, at the same time the more rejoicing is the more praying. Joy and prayer act and react in harmony with each other. To pray without ceasing implies that the voice is not an important element in prayer. The posture of prayer has no importance, it matters not how, if we stand, sit, lie on our face, or kneel down, it is the motives of the heart that matters to God. What the heart is thinking or saying, that is the bottom line when we pray to God. If we should always pray on our knees it would not be possible to pray without ceasing.

Listen to the psalmist when he said, 'Create in me a clean heart, O God, and renew a right spirit within me. Cast me not away from your presence, O God, and take not thy Holy Spirit away from me. Restore unto me the joy of thy salvation and renew a right spirit within me.'

If this is your cry, surely God will hear you. Sincere prayer is powerful and effective at all times.

IN TIMES OF PROSPERITY, our motives should remind us to pray. Solomon prayed and said, 'O Lord God of Israel, there is no God like you, in heaven above or on the earth below. You have kept your covenant of love with your servants who continue wholeheartedly in your way. You have also kept your promise to your servant David my father with your mouth, you have promise, and with your hands you have fulfilled it, as it is today' (1 Kings 8:22).

IN TIMES ADVERSITY, our motives should be prayer. The answer will come. James asks, 'Is any one of us troubled? We should pray. Is any one happy? He should sing. Is anyone sick? He should call the elders of the church to pray over him and anoint him with oil in the name of the Lord. And the prayer of faith will make the sick person well, and the Lord will raise him up. If he has committed any sins they will be forgiven him.' (James 5:13)

IN TIMES OF DANGER, we should remember that God is our protector. In the incident on the water, Peter was not putting Jesus to the test, but he was impulsive and his request led him to experience a rather unusual demonstration of God's power. Peter started to sink because he took his eyes off Jesus, and began to focus on the high waves. His faith wavered when he realized what he was doing. We may not all walk on water, but we do walk through tough situations. If we focus on the waves of difficult circumstances, we will surely go down. Rather, let us keep our eyes on Jesus who has the power over the angry waves (Matthew 14: 28; Luke 22: 42).

IN TIMES OF DARKNESS, our motives should be 'Jesus is my light and my salvation, whom shall I fear?' Jesus will send light. Jonah prayed from the belly of a fish to the Lord. He said, 'In my distress I called to the Lord, and he answered me. From the depth of the grave, I called for help, and he listened to my prayer.' Jonah thought that he was banished from the earth but he looked again toward God's holy temple. The Lord heard his cry and commanded the fish to vomit Jonah out on dry ground (Jonah 2:1). This shows us that prayer is profitable to the believer at all times, no matter if it is in the belly of our circumstances, our God will hear our prayer and come to our rescue. Prayer will put us into contact with our Father.

While Daniel was speaking, praying and confessing his sins and the sins of the people and making his request to the Lord, he prayed and said, 'Now Lord God, hear the prayer and the petition of your servant, for your sake, open your eyes and see the desolation of the condition of the city that bears your name. We do not make requests to God, because we are righteous, but because of your great mercy. O Lord listen, O Lord forgive, O Lord hear and act, for your name's sake. O Lord God, do not delay, because your city and your people bears your name.' While Daniel was praying he had a visitation from one of God's mighty angels, Gabriel, to tell him that he was highly esteemed, and that his prayers were answered. Just as how God answered as Daniel prayed we too can be confident that God will hear and answer our prayers (Daniel 9:23).

Prayer will acquaint God with our needs. Although Paul was in prison he was sent to encourage the believers to rejoice. He said, 'Rejoice in the Lord always, I will say it again, rejoice. Let your moderation be evident to all, the Lord is near. Do not be anxious about anything, but in everything by prayer and petition with thanksgiving present your request to God.' (Philippians 4: 4-7) Let us also take hold of this message and rejoice in the Lord.

Elijah had an encounter with the prophets of Baal at Mount Carmel. He prayed at the time of the sacrifice and said, 'O Lord God of Abraham, Isaac, and Jacob, let it be known today that you are God in Israel, and that I am your servant, and have done all these things at your command.' While he prayed the fire fell and burnt up the sacrifice, the wood, the stones, and the soil also licked up the water in the trench (1 Kings 18 36-39).

Prayer makes Satan tremble when he hears the weakest of saints on their knees. Therefore be 'strong in the Lord and in the power of His might. Put on the whole amour of God so that when the evil day comes, you may be able to stand your ground'. We are encouraged to put on the whole of amour of faith (Ephesians 5:10).

THE BELT OF TRUTH: Satan fights with lies, only the truth of God will defeat the lies of Satan.

BREASTPLATE of righteousness: Satan often attacks our heart which is the seat of our emotions, self-worth and trust.

THE FOOT WEAR is the readiness to spread the gospel. It would seem that telling others about the gospel is a tiresome task but God will strengthen our efforts as we go.

THE SHEILD OF FAITH will protect us from the enemy's flaming darts.

THE HELMET OF SALVATION will protect our minds from doubting what the word declares.

THE SWORD OF THE SPIRIT is the only weapon of offence in the list of armor. There are times when we need to take the offensive against the enemy, and remind him what the word of God says (Ephesians 6:10). These pieces of armor were designed especially for the believer to wear on their Christian journey. They are for protection from the darts of the enemy. The believer should not be absent minded and forget to put them on. They must be worn continually.

Join me in prayer.

O Lord, You are the Sovereign Lord who rules over all. You are great, greater than any other power of the universe. Father, You cannot be compared with any leader, preacher, government, governor of religion. O Lord, You alone are truly excellent.

Father, grant Your people a hunger and thirst for prayer and Your word. Create a thirst that not even natural water will satisfy; let only quenching of thirst come from drinking of that living water that we will never thirst again. Glory to God. Thank You, Jesus.

Father, thank You for the gift of salvation. Truly Lord, I do appreciate Your loving kindness and tender mercies. I am no more under the curse of sin, but I have been set free through the blood of Jesus Christ...

Amen

16

Beyond The Veil

Hebrews 9:16

Beyond the veil has shown significant events that symbolized Christ's work on the cross. Before the death of Christ the temple had three parts, namely: Firstly, the courts for all the people Secondly, the holy place where only the priest could enter once per year to make atonement for the sins of the people Thirdly, the most Holy Place where the Ark of the Covenant and God's presence with it, dwelled.

The renting of the veil signifies the revealing and the unfolding of the mysteries of the Old Testament. The veil of the temple was the concealment. It carried a harsh penalty for anyone to even take a glimpse in the Most Holy Place, where the Shekinah was. The renting of the veil means that Christ by His death opened a new way to God. Christ had offered Himself in the outer court, but His blood was now to be sprinkled upon the mercy-seat within the veil. Christ died so that the veil of guilt and wrath which was between God and man could be reconciled. Thank God for the free access through Christ to the throne of grace (Hebrews 9:16).

It also signifies the uniting of both Jews and Gentiles, and removing the partition wall that was between them. The ceremonial law had kept both apart. When Christ died He took it out of the way because the veil had kept people away from drawing near to God. What closeness there can be now that we can meet and greet each other, without the partition that was between us. Thank God the partition is taken out of the way and we can 'come boldly to the throne of grace' and find peace. Hallelujah!

The curtain that closed off the Most Holy Place from the view of the congregation was to conceal what was behind the veil. On the day of Christ death, when He cried out on the cross, the curtain was torn in two. The barrier that was between man and God was spilt in two. There was now entry for man to go to the Father in prayer for himself. Man can approach God directly through Christ at any time. We must pray earnestly until we reach beyond the 'veil'.

What is beyond the **veil**? When we get beyond the veil we will see ourselves as God sees us. When we look upon Jesus and look well into His wonderful face, the things of this world will grow strangely dim in the light of His glory and grace. We will experience the power of the Holy Ghost that lies beyond our natural thinking. Our eyes will be open to the 'truth'. We will have the ability to say 'not I that live, but the Christ that lives within me'. We will experience the Father of light, as He shines into our heart revealing Jesus the Son of God who came to ransom the world to Him, and destroy the works of the flesh.

Isaiah had a marvelous experience. He saw the Seraphim in the temple over the altar. He saw the Lord sitting upon a throne, high and lifted up, and His train filled the temple. Above it stood the Seraphim. Each one had six wings, and with two covered his face, and with two covered his feet, and with two flew. The Seraphim cry unto each another saying, '*Holy, Holy, Holy* is the Lord of host; the whole earth is full of His glory.' Isaiah noticed that the posts of the door moved at the voices of those that cried, and the house was filled with smoke.

After that experience Isaiah saw himself as a sinful man. He confessed and said, 'Woe is me for I am undone because I am a man of unclean lips and dwell in the midst of people with unclean lips, but now my eyes have seen the king, the Lord of host'.

Isaiah then describes how one of the Seraphim flew toward him with a piece of live coal that he took from off the altar and touched his lips. This indicates that his sin was taken away and he was purged. What a difference it must have made on Isaiah's part, when the weight of sin was lifted!

He was purged from his sins; he was now consecrated and ready to serve. He heard the voice of the Lord asking, 'Who shall I send? And who will go for us?' Isaiah was now in a right state of mind to accept the call and replied, 'Here am I, send me.' Isaiah was sent with a message to God's people. Isaiah was equipped with the ability to deliver God's massage to the people with boldness. At these times we can only respond to worship and glorify the Lord. In these times we will gain strength to face the battles of life. You will experience that after a period of meditation you will find grace to serve more effectively (Isaiah 6:1-5).

MOSES cried and said, 'Lord, if I have found grace in your sight show me thy way that I may know, that I may find grace in your sight, and consider that this nation is your people.' God granted Moses' request and said, 'My presence will go with you, and I will give you rest.' Moses still wanted to see the glory of the Lord. He asked, 'Please show me thy glory.' The Lord said to Moses, 'I will make all my goodness to pass before you, I will be gracious to you, and I will have compassion, but you cannot see my face, for no man shall see my face and live.' The Lord then directed Moses to hide behind a rock and said, 'while my glory passes by I shall cover you with my hand, then I will take my hand away that Moses will only see the back parts of God' (Exodus 33:13).

Here recorded is a glimpse into God's glory. We can visualize by faith into the throne room of heaven where God is sitting on His throne.

JOHN was shown a vision in the spirit that could not be seen by human eyes. He saw twelve tribes of Israel in the Old Testament and twelve apostles of the New Testament. The twenty-four elders in the vision may have represented all the redeemed of all times. The twenty-four elders show us how the redeemed of the Lord were worshipping

God. They were people from every nation and tribe and were praying before the throne, saying, 'Holy, holy is the Lord.' God's message of salvation is not limited to a specific culture, race, or country; it is free for all who ask.

Anyone who comes to God in repentance and faith is accepted by Him and will be a part of the Kingdom of God. It is part of the song that God's people sang as they praised Christ's work on earth: 'He was slain, He purchased them with His blood, He will gather them into a kingdom, and He has appointed us to reign on the earth.' As we recognize the greatness and faithfulness of God in our own lives, we too join the chorus of praise in declaring that 'The Lord is a great God and a great King above all gods' (Psalm 69:3).

We are blessed in the heavenly realms with every spiritual blessing in Christ. All that we long and hope for is found in a personal relationship with Jesus Christ. We yearn for and anticipate abundant life and God also yearns that we may develop into strong people of God to master His plans, and the ability that He has invested in us. He wants us to draw near to Him, so that He can draw near to us. He is no longer behind the hidden veil; we are allowed to go in and find Him. The way to God has been opened, it is clear and inviting, so that all may go in. Those who are hungry and thirst after righteousness will receive a Holy quench and the bread of life to sustain body, soul and spirit. *Come in. He bids you come...*

Jesus has already died and paid the penalty for sin. He has fulfilled God's requirement for the demands of the sins of the world. When

He cried on the cross 'It is finished', man's redemption had been paid. We worship God and praise Him for what He has done, what He is doing, and what He will do for all who trust Him. When we realize the glorious future that awaits us, we will find the strength to face our struggles (Revelation 4, 5).

One afternoon as I was meditating, a word dropped in my spirit that prayer was like 'a grater'. I decided to ponder the use of a grater. I discovered that a grater is used for making rough things smooth. For example grating a coconut, potatoes or any other ground provision when used, will give the produce a fine texture.

Therefore, prayer will make our lives like a refined texture; it will rub off the rough patches in our lives. The person who maintains a life of prayer will be transformed from roughness to smoothness, from confusion gentleness, to a peaceful personality, from darkness to light, from poor heath to wholesomeness, from death to live more abundantly.

Join me in prayer.

Thank You Jesus, praise God. Our loving God, we approach Your throne of grace and mercy, thanking You Lord, for such privilege that afford us to come boldly to Your Most Holiest of Place. Lord God Almighty, at one time we were far from You because of our wandering. Lord, we wandered far from home, but today we thank You for Your Holy Spirit that draws us back to You.

How wonderful is Your mercy. Father, we ask in the name of Jesus Christ to ever keep us near the cross at the precious fountain. Lord my God, we pray for a constant application of the blood of Jesus that we may always keep ourselves spotless from worldliness.

We again thank You for Your Son Jesus and it is in His name that we present our petitions.

Amen

17

Taking Our Place
In The Body Of Christ

The body of Christ can be termed 'the Church', a called out set of believers that makes up the church. The church is not a perfect organization. It is a geographically located, temporally limited and visibly evident as the body of Christ. In the very early New Testament days, the local church met in Jewish synagogues and had a very simple organization. Later the church met in homes (Romans 16: 5). It was not uncommon to have a number of churches in an area. The idea of meeting in a building constructed for the exclusive purpose is a New Testament idea.

We are called to a life of holiness. Therefore we are to make daily progress toward holiness through the blood of Jesus. He who calls us will perform the act of sanctification and spiritual discipline. It is a living spiritual house with Christ as the foundation and corner stone, and each believer as a stone. One stone is not independent of the other; one body part is useless without the other (1 Corinthians 12: 27).

When God calls one for a task we must be aware that He is also calling others with you. This is one of the reasons why all believes should live in the spirit of togetherness. All our efforts should be multiplied and be effective one toward another. When we the believer gave over our lives to the Lord we made a commitment to surrender to the Lordship of Christ. We automatically gave our life away to Christ at conversion. In the past we had lived a life of hopelessness, inadequacy, selfishness but thank God for Jesus. We have exchanged the old life for a new life in return for a life full of joy, hope, peace and security in Jesus.

Reason For Participation In The Local Church

The ultimate reason that we should participate in a local church is because it is specifically commanded by God. Even in the New Testament days there were those who yielded to the temptation of absent from the worship service of the local church. The writer of Hebrews points out that the member of a local church has an obligation to one another. We are to provoke one another to good works and to exhort one another to live consistent lives worthy of God.

Every believer should seek to occupy a place in the prayer life of the church. The church is like a recruiting centre. You will be given an assignment to accept the challenges and get into the position to carry out your duties with God's help. Our Christian duties must be done with integrity, wisdom, in patience and all the attributes that demand, love for Christ, love for our fellow-man, love for our enemies without favoritism. We must bear in mind that it is God who has graciously given us this unspeakable gift of salvation. We are privileged to belong to God's family, a community with Christ as the founder and foundation. Everyone in the community is related, we are brothers and sisters and we are loved equally by God. We should treat our families lovingly, although it will not be easy, but it is the best way to influence and introduce them to the love of God.

Each person should accept their responsibility and move into action. It was said that 'prayer is the life blood' of the church. Every believer should be engaged in the duty to pray regularly for themselves and for others. This method should be encouraged, as well as the significance of prayer, at the initial time of conversion, because a life that is built on prayer is a life that will be well equipped to withstand the test in times of trouble and during other calamities. As believers in the body of Christ we ought to know our leaders. We should acknowledge them as spiritual workers.

From time to time we should applaud and value our leaders. Jesus mentioned in Matthew 10: 42 that we should receive them as prophets. When we treat them as prophets we will receive a prophet's reward. And whosoever gives them even a cup of cold water, will not lose their reward. Leaders are called to labor; they work under pressure, with their brain and use of their muscles. They spend hours studying, in intense feeling and much unceasing toil. They rule in the name of the Lord, they are always in danger, and can come under attack and pressure when speaking out for the right. We must recognize the joint union of Christ and His church, and remember to hold our leaders up in our prayers.

The Minister In The Local Church

Although we all need to take our place, a minister that is ordained to manage a local church is one who has a pulpit ministry, who is called and commissioned by God to 'go into the entire world and preach the gospel, baptizing those who believe in the name of the Father, the Son and the Holy Ghost, teaching them to observe all things which he has commanded them' (Matthew 28: 19-29).

The duty of the minister of the gospel is to proclaim the truth. Whether it is received or not, he must never get discouraged with the results. He must do his duty well by planting and sowing seeds and leave the rest to God, who is responsible for the growth of the seeds. The minister is therefore called upon to remain faithful to his God. God is faithful to His word. He watches over His work to bring it to pass. He puts an extra premium on faithfulness. The man who hears the word has a written revelation of God. He must act on what he hears and live accordingly.

Every believer in reality is a minister in their own rights. One of the major tasks of the minister is to guide and develop those who do not have a pulpit ministry into the area of service. Paul told us that it was Christ who gave gifts to men. To some He gave apostles, some prophets, evangelist, some pastors and teachers. These gifts are to prepare God's people for service, so all believers are built up in the unity of the faith in the knowledge of the Son of God (Ephesians 4: 11-13).

I pray that the Holy Spirit will awaken every bishop, pastor, and layman to rise up and take their place in the body of Christ. Men of old were not afraid to weep before God on behalf of the people. A heart that is truly broken will yield the fruit of repentance and touch the hand of God for His mercy. They will cry, 'O Lord help, we need your help'.

Then our worship will be more effective and more souls will come to know the Lord as their Savior. Since the Bible makes it clear for those who are unprepared for the return of Christ, we then as believers are responsible to preach the message, to tell it, and live a godly life so that those who do not know the Lord, may be awakened to know the truth that will set them free.

Each believer has a responsibility to help other believers who are in need of developing their faith to become matured Christians. There is so much to be done in the body of Christ; but there is room for improvement, more faithful believers to engage in a life of prayer. We can also learn an important lesson to appreciate each other while there is time to do so. We should not wait for the final time when a person departs from the earth and when everyone is marching up to say how good the person was. My friend, would you say and agree with me that it might be too late? People should be supported and shown love when they are able to appreciate the appraisal, and not when they are unable. It is said that one should give flowers to persons while they can touch the petals, and smell the fragrance. God is pleased when we look after each other. We can recall that when the time comes for us to say goodbye to a loved one, listen to the things that is said about them… they cannot hear, see, or be touched by our good remarks, so try to do as many good while there is yet time. As the body is one, and has many members, and all the members of the body being many, are one body, so also is Christ's.

We could think of the human body as an analogy to establish this truth. A man is one person, even though he has various body parts, each with individual and separate parts. No individual part of the body can operate alone. So the church is made up of many persons regardless of cultural differences, or social statuses; those who drink of the Holy Spirit are melted together as one (John 7: 37).

We are God's special possession. We were bought with a price. It happens that the value of a thing is precious to the one who owns and possesses it, especially with a person of influence. It is the ownership that places the worth on a person or a thing. However precious and valuable a thing maybe, it is only the purchaser who can tell its worth… How valuable it is, how precious it is to the purchaser, that is who we are in God.

Each part of the body has a responsibility to function accordingly. God has no unused members. God has given each of us unique capabilities, and He has a place in His church for each of us to develop and use those gifts. It is important to find our place to serve to the best of our ability. It avails us nothing to spend time wishing we were in someone else's place. Why not consider who the Giver is, of these wonderful gifts and give Him thanks.

However, despite the emphasis on individual worth and usefulness everyone must still strive for unity within the body of Christ. Spiritual giftedness and strength is a precious gift from God to be used for His glory. Although there are many people within the same church, each have their own unique characteristics. God gives to each one gifts by the power of the Spirit. No one needs to feel he is not a part of the body.

There is no useless member in the physical body; neither should there be in the spiritual body of Christ. God has planned in His divine wisdom the body of Christ. The moment you are born into the body of Christ, you are automatically given a place in which to function. God is so kind and mindful to place gifts and talents in us to be developed and used for His glory.

If anyone wonders whether he has a place in the body of Christ, the answer is 'Yes, you have a place.' There is room for development and improvement to function effectively. Let us focus on the giver of gifts. God is the one who is so gracious and kind to give us special gifts to be used in His church, for the helping of each other. It has nothing to do with our intellectual ability, they all come from Him and through him, we have nothing to boast about like how clever we are, and what we can do.

The Benefits Of Participation In The Local Church

There are benefits to participation immediately apparent through those believers in Acts 20:7 who obeyed the command. They continued steadfast in the apostles' doctrine, they had fellowship, observance, breaking of bread, they participated in prayer, they enjoyed effective outreach, so that fear came upon every soul. They had a common cause, and had all things common. They had extra benefits of participation in the local church, worship, discipline and pastoral oversight (2 Corinthians 13: 1-10; Matthew 18: 15-17; 1 Peter 5: 1).

However, with this place comes responsibility, and with responsibility comes reward. If you do not take your place and function in the family of God in the church, the body will be weakened. God is looking for willing hearts that have a burning desire to take their place in His church. When we all find our place in the church and fill it effectively, the church will be strengthened greatly, and bring glory to God, not because we are filling our place but because everyone is doing their best in whatever their gift and calling demands.

Some have developed the idea that their special vocation is to criticize others for not doing their best. But it is the Holy Spirit who has this responsibility to be the judge, therefore we have no right in this matter, our business is to find our place and fill it effectively through prayer and reading and mediating on the word of God. Until we do this we are in serious trouble and will pay a price of negligence. It is advisable that we take our place in the body of Christ.

A healthy Christian church will grow in number when they see how we love one another; also in the community Christians will attract people to Christ when they see how Christians love and care for one another. Because of the love we show to others, it will have an impact, in homes, schools, colleges, and wherever there are people. There is nothing that can take God's love away from us; we have received His 'love marked' in our heart when we receive Christ as Lord of our lives.

Oh there is so much to be done! If we ever knew how much time there is for the Lord to return we would hurry up and find the courage to witness to everyone we meet. We may still have our children, friends, and love ones out there still not saved. What are you planning to do about this sin problem that is imprisoning our people? Let us join together and get busy to do what needs to be done.

Join me in prayer.

Heavenly, Father I come to You in the name of Jesus Christ and thank You for providing redemption through the death of Your Son. Father, I thank You that my life is spared to give You thanks. Thank You for the grace of Your unmerited favor that we did not earn. Father, help us to run this race with patience, looking to You who is the author and finisher of our faith.

O Father in heaven, we hallow Your great name that is above every other name. At this junction of my life I stand amazed, and wonder how You could love me, a sinner condemned. When I read from Your holy word how there is no more condemnation to them that are in Christ Jesus, who walk not after the flesh but after the Spirit, I raise my hands to You in praise and adoration.

Father, I bring the young and old before You. Please grant us Your peace that all may get along together in love, because You love us all and gave Your Son Jesus to die for us all – what a plan! Father, I thank You.

This I humbly ask in the name of Jesus Christ.

Amen

18

Developing Your Own Faith

What Is Faith?

Faith is the conviction based on past experience that God's new and fresh surprises will be ours. According to Hebrews 11: 1, 'Faith is the substance of things hoped for, the evidence of things not seen'. It takes strong faith to believe for things that cannot be seen or touched. It is through faith that we are saved and not by ourselves; it is the gift of God. Faith can be termed as the 'title deeds to what I was promised'. Our faith will be a substantial source of strength to recall previous experience of God's help. See the heroes of Faith in Hebrews chapter 11.

How Do We Develop Our Faith?

We should work our faith, or exercise our faith. We can draw from past experiences about the goodness of God; memorizing scripture verses pertaining to faith is useful. Trusting God that He is able to do exceedingly above what we may think or ask. We ought to seek ways of putting our faith to work, if our faith is weak, little, or struggling. Let us remember that God is able to build us up.

Will Our Faith Be Tested?

We have an example when King Jehoshaphat faced trouble from his enemies, that he prayed and called upon the God of his fathers and rehearsed past experiences of deliverance. The answer to his prayers came through with an assurance. 'Believe in the Lord your God, so shall you be established, believe his prophets, so shall you prosper' and he was delivered in an extraordinary victory. They were instructed to begin the warfare with an appeal to God and with prayerful acknowledgement of His own impotence, and then God would fight the battle through praise and thanksgiving in the valley of blessing (2 Chronicles 20 1-12).

It is necessary to have your own faith; prayer can develop your faith into strong working faith. While it is useful to master your own faith, it takes time for faith to grow. When trials appear, and the journey gets rough you will need your own faith to survive and having done all to stand. Faith in God will remove your mountains and deal with the goliaths that may try to invade our prayer space. How wonderful it is to be able to tap into your own faith.

If we should trust in the faith of others it will not be sufficient to stand in the evil times. The arms of flesh will fail; you dare not trust your own. Jesus said, 'Our faith will make us whole'. How God works on our behalf and His thoughts toward us demands genuine adoration and praise on our part. We must not forget to give God the highest praise for His providential care.

Everyone has the God-given ability to build his or her own faith. Some may float on carelessly until they are drawn into dangerous places, where there will be a test of faith. Our faith will be tested at times and we must demonstrate our confidence in God knowing very well that He will not lead us into darker places than He Himself has trod. We should build on the word of God, and take God at His word.

How To Deal With Test Of Faith

When we face our Jordon or hardship and discouragement, it is easy to lose sight of the bigger picture. We must keep in mind that we are not alone, there is help, and our help comes from the Lord. He will not allow us to go under. They that put their trust in the Lord shall be like Mount Zion that can never be moved.

To keep a proper perspective in the midst of difficulties is to keep in focus who is leading as we follow obediently. I often recall the story of the widow who wanted an answer from the king. Daily she would go to him; morning, noon and at night she went to see him until the king got very weary of her coming to him. One day when it seemed too much, the king decided to answer this persistent woman with her request. Brothers, sisters, and all the readers of this book, don't you believe that our Father is very pleased when we are persistent, going to

God in prayer. Let us go to Him regularly, not some times but all the time, be persistent. Go to God; He is waiting for you.

When we are going through our trials it can be compared to traveling through a subway. When you pass through a subway, you may be surrounded by darkness that is close and oppressive, however, you are always moving toward the light and fragrance of the open view. Likewise, it is important to remember that the darkness you face is not God's goals for your life. Instead, the tunnels are only a means to get somewhere else. The tunnel is not your abiding home; He is bringing you out into a larger place. As we keep our hand in God's, we are always sure to be moving toward Emmanuel's land where the sun shines and the birds always sing. God is ever guiding you the believer, sometimes with the delicacy of a glance, sometimes with the firmer grip of a ministry. He will move with you always, even through 'the valley of the shadow of death', God has promised to be there with His rod and staff to comfort you and me.

This is His message to help us in our earthly walk according to John 5: 7. Jesus said 'Herein am I glorified that ye bear much fruit.' The fruit of prayer will bear fruit by one of the branches and you and I are that branch. When we abide in Christ our life will be filled with joy. We should not allow anything or any one to prevent us from bearing fruit, life will not mean much outside of God's will. You don't need to make the same mistake that others make; the important lesson in life is to find oneself in the will of the Father.

You may ask, 'How do I worship in spirit and in truth?' God's Holy Spirit actively searches for those who will worship in childlike simplicity and praise. God never gives up; He continues to seek for those who will worship Him in spirit and in truth. This can be made possible by reading the word and putting the elements of prayer in action. Truth is also an important element in worship, for God is truth. When we acknowledge that God is truth it will bring us to a higher dimension, the truth will set us free.

I once read a story about some ministerial students who were visiting a church. While they were waiting for the doors to be open, a man approached and asked, 'Would you like to see the heating apparatus of the church?' They thought how queer his question was, to want to show them the heating system but they agreed, and following him they came to a door. He quietly opened it and whispered, 'There sirs, is our heating apparatus.' Inside the room there were about some hundred intercessors kneeling in prayer, seeking an outpouring of God's Spirit upon the service which was soon to begin. *This is a true story and the unknown guide was Spurgeon himself.*

Strive To Become Mature In Our Faith (2 Peter 3: 18)

We are admonished to grow in grace and in the knowledge of our Lord and Savior Jesus Christ. When we think of the word 'grow' it means to increase. To grow is to mature from childhood to adulthood. To grow is a gradual process. Even in friendship, it grows much stronger and more precious, especially in the Christian faith, over time. Our Father delights in His children when they grow in grace and show good respect of becoming fully matured Christians. Those who do not grow will become stunted and always remain on the diminishing side.

If we feed our minds on God's word, we will become champions. The word is sometimes referred to as milk, bread, wine, meat, water and honey. As young Christians we would desire the sincere milk of the word. As we begin to grow we will desire to start eating harder stuff, like meat. In the spiritual sense we should strive to be mature where we can enjoy the fullness of God's program for our lives. It is said that milk is for the babies, strong meat is for grown ups (1 Peter 2: 2).

Some people will only base their Christian philosophy on the observance of the Ten Commandments and make a full stop. But there are many more commandments in the Bible that are just as important as the others. Therefore, spiritual maturity is important in order to grow into the likeness of Christ. The lack of maturity in the believer will result in an ineffective ministry to other Christians. We should seek to edify each other through the word and with prayer. The word of God when applied will allow us to become a channel through which the ministry can flow from one Christian to another.

Jesus admonished His followers to 'come after Him, and he will make them fishers of men' (Mark 17: 1). This call requires no special ability, just a willingness and faith to obey. Therefore we have a mandate to fish for souls, and to win them to Christ. They are lost in the sea of life. There are often danger zones on the sea of life but the call is 'fish until you find'. How wonderful it is to rescue others from the coldness of sin, and bring them into the warmth of the family of God where they can be nurtured and receive love and fellowship. Then as soon as they are strong enough they themselves will be taught the same lesson to become fishers for men. The command goes on and on until Jesus returns.

We are admonished to rid our minds and hearts from bitterness, strife, anger, and any other immature behavior that would stop our growth in Christ Jesus. And for heaven's sake, let us grow on to maturity.

Here are some facts that will help to build your own faith to enable you to pray effectively:

- Read the word of God with anticipation. Believe what the word says.

- Find scriptures on faith, read, and meditate on them.

- We are to pray and ask the Lord to increase our faith.

- The word is for you. It is as though there is no other person in the world but you, and the revelation has been given especially to you. You can say with full assurance, 'It is mine' and then say it again, until it sinks way down into the recesses of your heart.

- No one has more right to it than you have.

- Develop a humble spirit; it makes no sense to be proud and haughty.

- Every promise in God's word is yours; He is talking to you.

- You can say 'He is my Father, and I am His child.'

- Be careful for nothing, but in everything let us make our request be known.

19

A Mother's Story

A mother once told a true story that while praying for one of her children in the early hours of the morning, as she travailed in prayer asking God to intervene in the life of her son, for his conviction and to turn to God, she was confident that her prayer was heard. She recognized that she had no power, strength, or might to save her son; so she went in prayer to the One who can give help. She devoted extra time to ask God to allow His will to be done in the life of her son. She prayed with an expectation that God was constantly watching, and listening to her prayer. As soon as she began to get deeper in praying, she felt a kind of courage to declare, '*God, You are my possibility*'.

In her final word in prayer she whispered, 'Lord, I am resting on your word in faith.' A few hours later she heard the phone ring and wondered who could be calling at that time of the morning. She quickly picked up the receiver, 'Hello, good morning' the voice echoed.

She held her breath and listened again as the voice said in a calmer manner, 'Hello Mother. Mother, all is well?'

She replied 'All is well with me, my son, and what about you?' He answered, 'Yes mother it is well with me, I just thought of giving you a call before you do your devotion. I know that it is about this time of the morning you would be praying.' She said, 'I was just lifting you up in prayer and calling your name to the Lord...for your soul salvation.'

'One day when the time comes God will call me,' he said in a low voice. He continued 'Mother, nothing is done before the time. I will give up one of these days.' He then assured her: 'Mother, did you know that I pray and read my Bible almost every day?'

His mother replied, 'But son, that is not all that is required, there must be a surrender, a confession and believing in Jesus. You must acknowledge Jesus as your personal Savior and Lord of your life.'

She thought, might just as well I give him the whole truth, this is a good opportunity, because normally he would always be in a hurry having ten things lined up that he had to do. Sure enough he replied, 'But wait a minute mother, not so fast, we will get to that another time. I have some loose ends that I need to tie up, but certainly I will give it some thought.'

The mother felt in her spirit that something was happening to her son more than natural. She knew in her spirit that her son was resisting the spirit of conviction and refusing to give himself to the

Lord; however she replied, 'Son, God is always calling you, but you are not listening to His voice.' She decided to tone down and wish him a good day and reassured her son of how much she loved him, and that she would continue praying for him.

As this mother pondered within her spirit she said, 'I wonder what is happening to my son, I hope that he is ok. This could be the very thing that I am praying to hear him say.' All kinds of thoughts crossed her mind for normally that son would never ring this time of the morning; it was so unusual and very strange. She thought, I wonder if he is alright. She had not heard from her son for a while, and was concerned, however she encouraged herself that there is nothing that God cannot deal with. She thought 'I will continue praying that one day, he will to surrender himself to the higher power of Almighty God.'

She continued to stretch her faith, and placed a copy of her son's picture in her bedroom, another one she placed in her Bible as a reminder that whenever she goes to church and prayer meetings to pray for her son. She would often ask her close prayer partners to remember her son when they prayed, knowing that the effectual fervent prayer of a righteous man will avail much. She placed another picture of him in her prayer room, and believed him to be surrounded by prayer no matter where he lives and travels.

Although the son has not yet surrendered his life to the Lord, she confessed that she has enough faith and patience to wait on the Lord. Her duty is to keep on praying for her son and for others like him. It is the Lord who does the drawing, and the saving. No man can come to Him unless the Father draws them. They that wait on the Lord shall renew their strength, they shall mount up with wings as eagles, they shall run and not be weary, and they shall walk and not faint. *Bless the Lord.*

The mother declares that her expectation is in God who changes things and people. She praises the Father with a grateful heart, and believes that in due time God will save her son. She remembered the word of God that says, 'He is a rewarder to them who seek Him diligently.' She decided not to cease praying for her son, and every time her son would call, or visit, during his conversation with his mother he would say, 'Mother, please keep on praying for me for I can feel your prayers.' The son told his mother that sometimes he would find himself in some difficult situations but he was confident that she was constantly praying for him. He has also mentioned to his friends how his mother prays for him every day. Some of his friends ask that his mother remember them too in her prayer.

This faithful mother believes that when God is ready to draw both her son and his friends, it will be a time of revival. That will be a time of rejoicing for what God has done, so in the mean time she said that she is beginning to shout because she believes that it won't be long when her prayers will be answered. I would like you too as you read about this situation to join in prayer for this mother and her son, that God will soon intervene and save him and his friends in Jesus Christ's name. And perhaps you have a similar condition struggling with? I would like you to remember that God is not slack concerning His promise as some men would count slackness, but He is faithful to His promise. Because the promise is for us and our children's children, and as many as the Lord our God shall call (Acts 2: 9). **Let us claim the promise**.

Join me in prayer.

Father God, how good and gracious You are! Words are not enough to express my gratitude to You. Thank You for helping me to complete this book. Father, only You know the disappointments and struggles I had to face while putting the pages together. Father, You see the stops and starts I had to make, but nevertheless I came this far by faith, leaning on Your promises.

Thank You for the skills, ability, and the words that You have put in my spirit every time to put pen to paper. When Your inspiration comes over me to search the scriptures, and to write, it is amazing. I thank You again for the strength in my fingers, my eyes, and the whole of me. When at times I feel like making a full stop and calling it a day, You gave me another chance to carry on.

Thank You for touching my eyes especially when they are filled with tears of gratitude. O Lord, I thank You for granting my readers Your mercy and goodness; let these virtues follow us all the days of our lives.

Lord, You have seen in my heart at times when I search the scriptures and identify my sins, my faults, and my failures on the pages of Your word, how much I get anxious. Thank You for a lively conscience that aroused me to pray and ask for Your forgiveness and cleansing for every sin that I know of and those that I cannot remember.

What can I say Lord, but to praise and live for You more and more until I lose myself and find it all in Your grace. Father, thank You. I ask these mercies in Jesus Christ's name.

Amen

20

Miscellaneous

The Names of God Chart

Name	Meaning	Reference	Significance
Eholim	God	Genesis 1:1	Refers to God's power and might
Yahweh	The Lord	Gen 2:4	The Hebrew name of a divine person
El-Elyon	God Most High	Gen. 14 :17-20	He is above all gods
El-ROI	God Who Sees	Gen. 16:12	God over sees all creation, and the affairs of people
El-Shadai	God Almighty	Gen. 17:1	God is all powerful
El-Olam	The Everlasting God	Isaiah 40:28-30	God is eternal, He will never die

252 Phyllis Jemmott

Yahweh	The Lord Will Provide	Gen. 23 13-14	God will provide our real need
Yahweh-Nissi	The Lord Is My Banner	Exodus 17:15	We should remember God for helping us
Adonai	Lord	Due. 6:4	God alone is the head over all
Yahweh-Elohe	Lord God Of Israel	Judges 5:3	He is God of the nation
Y-Isreal-			
Yahweh-Shalom	The Lord Is Peace	Judges 6:24	God give us peace so we need not fear
Qedosh-Yisrael	Holy One Of Israel	Isaiah 1:4	God is morally perfect
Yahweh	The Lord Of Host	I Sm. 1;3	God is our savior and protector
Yahweh-Tsidkenu	The Lord Is Our Righteousness	Jeremiah 23:6	God is our standard for right behavior

A Guide to Effective Prayer

Yahweh-Shammah	The Lord Is There	Ezekiel 48:35	God is always present with us
Attiq_ Yomi n	Ancient Of Days	Daniel 7:9 13:12	God is the ultimate authority, He will one day judge all nations

I find that the names of God are important and we should know the meanings and what they signify to us.

In the Old Testament times the people of God were acquainted with the different names of God, and so for us who are in this age of grace it is good to know the names and their meanings as well.

Join me in prayer.

Lord God of heaven, there is none like You in heaven and in the earth. Lord, You are eternal and cannot fail, and cannot die: we give you praise. You give us peace that we have no need to fear, how excellent is Your power and might. Lord, You are ever present among Your people; we thank You for Your concern over our lives, for truly we could not keep ourselves, not even if we tried.

We pray heavenly Father, please increase our faith. Lord when we want to do what is right, evil always present itself, so Father please be near us at all times that we may never surrender to the evil one.

Lord God of heaven, we cry out to You for help. In the evil days that are ahead of us, Father, always remember to keep our hearts in perfect peace and our mind stayed on You. Lord, please guide and shield us from the enemy, that we may keep focus on Your goodness.

Remember our children in other parts of the world, who may be facing attack. Lord, please draw near and deliver them. We want to say how good You are to our children; Your mercies never fail, and thank You again for the wonderful gift of life.

We humble ask these mercies in Jesus Christ's name.

Amen

Some Extras

This message was sent to:
A faithful Steward

You are a brilliant man with exceptional knowledge in both world affairs and spirituality. You have developed an excellent ability to balance financial and life resources in a Godly manner. Through the grace of God you are blessed with an honest spirit and an outstanding character. You have served in a very technical capacity for many years as an accountant. It is reported that at the end of such period, you were found to be trustworthy.

You have demonstrated that one can be in charge of little or large amounts without yielding to temptation. You have set good examples by giving clear definition in details of how you have managed church funds. It was a good report. One can recall listening keenly when you read the church notices, how your words were clear and concise, and easy to understand.

You are blessed with a God-given ability to handle anything from a dollar to millions without being in question... *What a remarkable man of God you are!*

You have passed the test in stewardship with flying colors. You are a good planner, good bookkeeper, good change giver, and a financial expert.

You have received your training in the school of *'Accountability'*.

You have developed in further studies in the college of *'Integrity'*.

You have gained a Masters degree in *'Faithfulness'*.

In addition, you are now working in the field of *'Trustworthiness'*.

Your dearest wife and children count themselves blessed to have you as their leader.

May God bless you as you embark on the most exciting and important journey... your Christian journey. I will be constantly praying for you.

This message was sent to a young person: A Notable Person

Your inner beauty permeates on the outside as to say '*all is well*'. You have an eye- catching smile that makes others want to join in and smile too, regardless of the weather condition, or circumstances. Your smile tells a story, of how you are inside… keep on smiling…You have an excellent personality that draws people to you. When persons are in your company they can feel the glow of happiness that is coming from you.

You have the ability of a leader who has the ability to hold an audience together, regardless of age or back ground. You have demonstrated good influence among peers by your creativity and the ability to put your words together in order to make sense.

You believe that in the academic world there is plenty room at the top therefore that is where you are making plans to be. You are well aware that getting at the top will require discipline, and knowing who you are and who you believe in. God has given you this assurance that nothing is impossible with Him; He knows no limit. With this in mind you believe that nothing can stop you reaching your full potential. You are also aware that nothing can take the place of persistency, talent will not. But the persistency of a person to whom God has blessed is most crucial. Be patient with yourself and remember that life is a process.

When you think of five years from now, you are excited, encouraged, and can exaggerate because you will then be nearing the top of your career. At that point you will be in a position to give commands and be the leader that was waiting to take up position.

In your quiet moments it is important to read the word of God so that it can continue to take you through the various stop and go signs. You will find the direction that you will need for the next level.

My prayers are that God will grant you the ability to complete academically and spiritually, for both will produce a balance to your life.

This message was sent to:
A man with Double-Edge Ability

You are from a generation of 'heroes' who specialize in 'goodness and 'mercy. Your coming into the world was not a mistake. You were born for a specific purpose and destiny. You were pulled from the crowd of many people like yourself but you were specially called to be a vessel unto the Lord. Therefore you could not escape from the mighty 'pull towards your assignment'. Your finishing will be more exciting than your beginning, it is more challenging, more searching in anticipation...

You believe that there is no one so strong to stop you from developing into the person who God said you are... you are certainly going places. You cry like the apostle Paul, 'O the riches and magnitude of the grace of God, it is unsearchable.'

Your testimonies and your life experiences have helped you through the many ups and downs of life. These are real issues that people face on a daily basis. Through it all you have demonstrated courage and compassion, and now you are eager to see persons free from the burden of sin.

Your preaching ministry has taken you far and near. You have met with people of both high and low intelligence. Nevertheless God has imbued you with special ability to minister to everyone you come in contact with. You have the corporation of the 'Divine Trinity' with you wherever you travel. They are your constant companions. Your messages are deep and soul searching. They have the power and anointing to convict men of sin, and also help them to build their lives again.

I pray that heaven's breeze will engulf you as you peruse in your endeavourer to preach, teach, and live well without compromise.

This was sent to: A unique man of God

Although you are highly qualified in so many areas, in education, spirituality in ministry, you are noted to be a man of a 'humble spirit'. It is apparent that you have not depended on your knowledge alone, but you seek the wisdom and knowledge that comes from God, who gives liberally. You are genuine and have a conviction that is concrete, stable; it is attached to the Rock, which is Jesus.

You are a people person and you will reach persons at any level to bring them up from where they may be. You have the ability to preach the word and even give it in bite sizes so that people of any age can understand your message of hope. You are never afraid to share your vision with others, even if it means that they will run with it before you have the chance to implement it. You are not at all perturbed, because you have the blue print, the original, and that is what counts.

In the race you will be exposed to opposition and critics; all these are negativities that will only strengthen your character and give you the power to cross the finishing line.

You preach the word under the anointing of the Holy Sprit which allows you to leave no stones unturned. You minister to the whole man, to body, soul, and the spirit. You have developed an understanding about people that sometimes they might need a chance to try again and maybe even a second chance. But with the level of patience that God has invested in you it is evident that person will accept the message and turn to God. Your messages are prepared with people in mind, they are soaked in prayer, faith, fasting, and the anointing that destroys the yoke and will undo heavy burdens; that is one of the reasons why your messages can be reflected on days after they were delivered.

Your lovely wife and children are proud of you; you are a special part of their lives.

I pray that you will receive freshness from God in your inner being as you continue to do your best to serve the Lord. We will reap what we have sown. He will pay a good wage when He shall return.

A Guide to Effective Prayer REFERENCES & BIBLE SCRIPTURES USED

The Lord's Prayer Matthew 6

Kinds of Prayer:

Secret Matthew 6:6 Family Acts 10:2-30. Groups Matthew 14:20 Public Corinthians 14:14-17

Parts of Prayer:

Adoration Daniel 4:34-35 Confession 1John 1:9 Supplication Timothy 2 1-3 Intercession James 14-15 Thanksgiving Philippians 4:6

Personal Requirements of:

Purity of heart Psalms 66 18-19 Believing in Christ's name John 14:13 According to God's will John 5:14

General requirements of:

Forgiving spirit Matthew 6:14 Simplicity Matthew 6:5-6 Humility and repentance Luke 18 10-14 Tenacity Luke 18 1-8 Importunity Luke 115-8 Intensity Matthew 7:7-11 Confident expectation Mark 11:24 Without many words Matthew 6:7 Unceasing Thessalonians 5:17

Answers refused because of:

Sin Psalms 66:18 Selfishness James 4:3 Doubt James 1 5-7
Disobedience Proverbs 28:9 Inhuman Luke 18:11

Join me in prayer.

Jesus, You are the center of my joy. O God and Father, in the name of Jesus Christ I come in Your presence, for there is fullness of joy and at Your right hand, there is pleasure for evermore. Lord, You are gracious, lovely and wonderful. We praise Your holy name. Father, You are awesome, and the heavens declare Your glory.

Jesus, how great Thou art. Holy Spirit, You are such a comfort to us, we love You, adore You, we bow down before You. Holy Spirit of God, breathe on us as You did on the disciples on the day of Pentecost. We long for You my God and Savior. Come Holy Spirit come, and take Your place with us.

Lord, let Your virtue enfold us through the blessed name of Jesus Christ. We ask You to visit our friends across the world and remind them of the grace that has brought them thus far. Let them ever be mindful of Your great salvation which You have offered to whosoever will.

We ask these mercies in Your great name, the name of Jesus Christ.

Amen

Conclusion

I conclude this journey with great appreciation to Almighty God who has helped me during the preparation of this book.

Each chapter of this book was written with my readers in mind. I hope that this book will inspire you as it did to me. Each time when I typed on the computer, it involved my whole being; many of the nights as I wrote and rewrote the pages, I could sense the Holy Spirit strengthening me with deep thoughts from within.

As I searched the scriptures it brought new insights to my spirit and to my mind. The word of God became more alive to me; it increased my desire to stay in the word and in prayer all the time.

Writing this book has brought a well into my spirit that flows from a deeper source of satisfaction within me. I personally give thanks to God that my sins are forgiven, all my guilt is erased and the world looks much brighter.

I pray that reading A GUIDE TO EFFECTIVE PRAYER has worked for you, as it did for me.

And this I pray, that your love may abound still more in knowledge and all discernment... that you may approve the things that are excellent, that you may be sincere and without offence till the day of Christ.

I pray that you may be filled with the fruit of righteousness, to the Glory and praise of God. Philippians 1:9–11

In Jesus Christ's name. Amen.

Acknowledgements

I must first thank the Father, the Son, and the Holy Spirit for inspiration, strength and courage to finally finish writing this book. Without them I would not be able to say hitherto has the Lord helped me.

I would like to take this opportunity to thank my husband Charles, affectionately called David, for his help and support in searching the scriptures.

God richly bless you.

To France, my spiritual daughter, for her support. She has been very instrumental in many ways. Thank you so much; I could not complete this book without your support.

To Barbara, my cousin, who read the first draft of the book. Thank you so much.

Bibles versions used: The Open Bible and The New International Bible

Commentaries: Evangelical 1981-1982
By: Phyllis Jemmott 2009

Join me in prayer.

Loving God, I come to You in the blessed name of Your Son Jesus Christ. I give You thanks. I ask Your forgiveness and cleaning in the name of Jesus Christ. Father, please teach me Your way and how to love. O Father, I need You so much. Lord, I ask You to consider me. Come and fill me with Your divine Presence that I might know how to give true worship. Lord, sometimes when I pray I can still feel that there are more gaps to be filled in my life. Lord, open my eyes to Your truth that I may always hunger for more of You.

Remember those who are going through trials. I ask of You to give them the necessary strength to stay faithful, by referring to The Guide to Effective Prayer.

Father, I give You special thanks for helping me to complete this book. It has been my heart beat over the years of preparation. I do appreciate Your inspiration that You gave from time to time. Truly, Father, I could never have had the strength and determination to go on without Your help. At times You saw how tired I was, but Father I looked to You for strength in those moments. I can now walk with my head high, not in pride, but because I am confident that You were there for me all the time. I ask this in Jesus Christ's name... Halleluiah.

Amen

Lightning Source UK Ltd.
Milton Keynes UK
UKOW04f1925221114

242014UK00002B/5/P